D1571657

KAMEN NEVENKIN

# FROM BESSARABIA TO BELGRADE

## AN ILLUSTRATED STUDY OF THE SOVIET CONQUEST OF SOUTHEAST EUROPE,

### MARCH - OCTOBER 1944

© PeKo Publishing Kft.

**PUBLISHED BY**
PeKo Publishing Kft.
8360 Keszthely, Bessenyei György utca 37.
Email: info@pekobooks.com
www.pekobooks.com

**RESPONSIBLE PUBLISHER**
Péter Kocsis

**AUTHOR**
Kamen Nevenkin

**EDITOR**
Tom Cockle

**LAYOUT**
Adam Nagy / nadam.hu

**PRINTED IN HUNGARY**

**FIRST PUBLISHED**
2020

ISBN 978-615-5583-28-5

# TABLE OF CONTENTS

# CHAPTER 1

# INTO RUMANIA

## CRISIS IN THE UKRAINE AND BESSARABIA

The Red Army reached northeastern Rumania in the last days of March 1944. Stalin and his aides had high hopes that the Fronts of Marshal Konev (2nd Ukrainian) and Army-General Malinovsky (3rd Ukrainian) would be able to quickly advance towards Bucharest, the Ploesti oilfields and the Bulgarian border. But those hopes were not meant to be fulfilled. Despite the heavy political pressure and the repeated Allied bombing raids, Rumania did not capitulate. Instead, Marshal Antonescu, the Rumanian dictator and supreme commander, sent more divisions to the northeastern front where they, together with the experienced veteran formations of the German Army Group "South Ukraine", repelled several Soviet offensives. Stalin was not keen to give up his ambitions to conquer the Balkans already in the spring of 1944, but after the fiasco at Târgu Frumos in early May he was finally forced to acknowledge the truth that Rumania would not fall and ordered Konev and Malinovsky to switch over to the defensive. The Soviet conquest of the Balkan lands had to be postponed for four months.

\* \* \*

The grandiose offensive that brought the Red Army to the gates of the Balkans was unleashed in the first week of March 1944. Stalin's strongest ground formations – 1st Ukrainian Front of Marshal Zhukov, 2nd Ukrainian Front of Marshal Konev and 3rd Ukrainian Front of Army-General Malinovsky delivered powerful blows over the course of three consecutive days and slowly, but steadily began to push the Germans out of the Ukraine.

In the north Zhukov advanced in the general direction of the Carpathian Mountains and the former Polish province of Galicia. By the end of the month his forces successfully created a large pocket in the vicinity of Kamenets-Podolsk, trapping more than 200,000 troops of the German 1. Panzer-Army inside. Nevertheless, the commander of that army, *General der Panzertruppe* Hans Hube (a Stalingrad survivor), didn't lose his head and launched a breakout. Guided by the clever orders of his immediate superior, *Feldmarschall* von Manstein (the Commander-in-Chief of Army Group "South"), Hube attacked in the direction least expected by Zhukov and his divisions quickly overran the thin Soviet blocking positions in the northwestern perimeter. By 10 April, in close coordination with the fresh German relief forces attacking from the northeast, the entire 1. Panzer-Army was able to fight its way out. However, the success came at a cost. The twenty or so divisions that were rescued had to leave behind nearly all their heavy weapons and equipment. Now they were nothing more than mere shadows of their former selves that required thorough reconstitution.

Manstein's decision to change the direction of Hube's breakout from southwest, toward Rumania, to northwest, toward Lwów, was based on the realization that 1. Panzer-Army would end up pressed back into the Carpathian Mountains, whereas it was more important to rejoin with the German forces in Galicia. Eventually, it did help stabilize the crumbling German front in the former Polish southeastern provinces. It did, however, mean that the Axis forces retreating into Rumania to the south of "Hube's pocket" were now seriously weakened, and this happened at the time when the officials in Bucharest were in secret negotiations with the Allies over a peace treaty.

Even though Zhukov failed to destroy 1. Panzer Army, he achieved a major operational success. His 1st Tank Army crossed the Dniester River and reached the town of Chernovtsy at the slopes of the Carpathian Mountains, thereby effectively severing the ground communications of Hube's 1. Panzer Army with its neighbor to the south, 8. Army of *General der Infanterie* Otto Wöhler. As a result, Army Group "South" was de facto split into two unequal parts divided by the Carpathians. The northern one was re-designated Army Group "Northern Ukraine", while the southern one (the former Army Group "A") became Army Group "Southern Ukraine". These new designations were a bit strange, because by then a very small portion of the Ukraine had remained in German hands. Furthermore, with the severing of the Tarnopol-Proskurov railroad the Soviets had effectively cut off the main supply lifeline of Army Group "South Ukraine". Now, the southernmost German army group was forced to use the long roundabout route through Rumania, where the railway network was less dense and in poor condition.

Although he personally presented Hube the Diamonds to the Knight's Cross, Third Reich's highest military decoration, Hitler considered the withdrawal from the Ukraine a major defeat. 1. Panzer-Army had not escaped yet, when on 30 March Hitler's personal four-engine plane picked up both Manstein and *Feldmarschall* Ewald von Kleist, the Commander-in-Chief of Army Group "A", and flew them to the "Eagle's Nest" in Berchtesgaden for a meeting. Upon receiving them, the Fuehrer awarded both marshals with Swords to their Knights Crosses and then immediately sacked them from their posts. His argument was that the time for regular military operations had gone and what was in great demand now were commanders who could stand fast. Manstein was succeeded by *Feldmarschall* Walter Model, while Kleist was replaced by Generaloberst Ferdinand Schörner, the commander of 17. Army.

## KONEV STRIKES

On 5 March the recently promoted Marshal Konev launched his grand offensive against the German 8. Army under General Wöhler. After five days of heavy fighting in very difficult conditions (an early thaw had set in turning the entire area into a sea of mud) the Soviets took the town of Uman, the principal supply and logistic base of Army Group "South". Large quantities of booty were seized, including several big military stores crammed with various goods, as well as hundreds of non-operational panzers and self-propelled guns that the Germans had failed to evacuate from the workshops.

*Marshal Konev and Marshal Rotmistrov in a command post during the invasion of Rumania, the spring of 1944. (Author's collection)*

One of those who witnessed the German collapse firsthand was the Russian-born Alexander Werth, BBC War Correspondent assigned to the Red Army. Some twenty years after the event he wrote the following:

It was soon after the liquidation of the Korsun "bag" and on the day after Konev's capture of Uman that I had the good fortune of being the only Western foreign correspondent authorized to visit the 2nd Ukrainian Front, where I spent one of the most illuminating weeks of all my war years in the Soviet Union. […]
The "Mud Offensive" was in full swing. It was one of the most extraordinary things that had happened; it was contrary to all rules of warfare. Barely three weeks after the liquidation of the German troops trapped at Korsun, Konev had struck out at a time when the Germans had least expected it. So deep and impassable was the Ukrainian mud. […]

The Ukrainian mud in spring has to be seen to be believed. The whole country is swamped, and the roads are like rivers of mud, often two feet deep, with deep holes to add to the difficulty of driving any kind of vehicle, except a Russian T-34 tank. Most of the German tanks could not cope with it. […]

The Germans assumed that while the Schlammperiode - the deep-mud period - continued, there was nothing to fear, and, mobilizing thousands of Ukrainian civilians, they were busy fortifying their new line north of Uman.

It was on March 5, with the mud and "roadlessness" at their worst, that Konev started his fantastic "Blitzkrieg through the Mud". It started with a gigantic artillery barrage against the German lines; within six days, the Germans were driven forty miles back, and chased out of Uman. The mud was such that they abandoned hundreds of tanks and trucks and guns, and fled - mostly on foot - to Uman and beyond. At one railway station the Russians captured a newly-arrived train with 240 brand-new tanks. Usually, however, the Germans burned or blew up both lorries and tanks.

Although Russian tanks were able to advance through the mud, the artillery lagged behind; and it was very often a case of Russian infantry, sometimes supported by tanks, but sometimes not, pursuing German infantry. Konev's Mud Offensive was "against all the rules", and the Germans had certainly not expected it. The Russian infantry and tanks rapidly advancing to the Bug and beyond - and, before long, towards Rumania – were being supplied with food, munitions and petrol by a large number of Russian planes.

These also did some strafing of German troops, and would have done more but for the weather. The only vehicles, apart from T-34 tanks, that advanced fairly successfully through the mud were the Studebaker trucks, for which the Russian soldiers were full of praise.

Very striking, as I was to discover in the next few days, was the high morale of the Russians and the poor morale of the Germans, who had been unnerved by the Korsun disaster, by the suddenness of Konev's March 5 offensive and by the loss of practically all their heavy equipment.

With the permission of General Konev, the Major and I flew in two tiny U-2 planes from Rotmistrovka to Uman the next day. […]

Then we circled over a plain: hundreds of German helmets still lay about, but all bodies had been buried; and soon the grass would grow over the many thousand Germans who had been slaughtered here. Next came several lines of trenches - these had been German trenches till March 5.

Having crossed these shattered German lines, we flew for many miles over roads that presented the strangest spectacle. They were cluttered up with thousands of burned-out lorries, and hundreds of tanks and guns, which the Germans had abandoned in their panicky retreat through the mud. And this strange, static procession of burned-out vehicles stretched all the way to Uman.

The day we arrived Uman presented a fantastic sight. One large building in the centre of the town was still smoldering. The streets were crammed with burned-out German vehicles, and were littered with thousands of papers, trodden into the mud, office records, private documents and letters, photographs, and also whole bundles of well-printed colored leaflets in Ukrainian exalting the "German-Ukrainian Alliance". One said "Down with Bolshevism" and showed a manly hand in a green sleeve tearing down a red flag with the hammer-and-sickle; another showed a German soldier shaking hands with another person in an unrecognizable pearl-grey uniform. "Our alliance will give happiness to all the nations of Europe"; still another called "Oath to the Fatherland" showed a crowd of gallant horsemen raising their arms to heaven and swearing: "None will lay down his arms while our Ukraine is enslaved by the Bolsheviks." [1]

After the taking of Uman the frontage of Konev's offensive increased to 300 km. On 12 March his forward detachments crossed the southern Bug River, which had formed the border between the German-occupied Ukraine and the Romanian-occupied part of Ukraine, called Transnistria. This was made possible mainly because at the village of Khashchuvate the fleeing Germans had failed to demolish the bridge across the river. [2]

On 18 March the Soviets forced another wide river - the Dniester - and, wasting no time, began to expand their bridgehead on the western bank. The Axis forces opposing them were totally demoralized by the defeat and could offer very little, if any, resistance. They not only had abandoned their heavy equipment, but some of them even tossed away their personal weapons and small arms. Some of the Germans and Rumanians were so panicked and terrified that they arrived in Bessarabia bare-footed and half-naked. [3]

1   A. Werth, "Russia at War 1941-1945", New York, E. P. Dutton & Co, 1964.
2   Tsentralnyi Arhiv Ministerstva Oborony, fund 240, inventory 2779, folder 873, page 16. (Hereafter cited as TsAMO, fu. 240, inv. 2779, f. 873, p. 16.).
3   Ibid., pp. 16-17.

The sorry sight of the utterly defeated enemy impressed even a battle-hardened veteran like Konev. He wrote in his memoir that

> the Germans were not merely defeated, they fled from the Ukraine naked, without their artillery, Panzers and motor transport. They fled on oxen, cows, even on foot, and abandoned all their equipment.[4]

Konev was quite right. The German reports from the period in question indicate that even their most prominent formations, the panzer-divisions, were down to almost nothing in terms of heavy weapons and equipment. Thus by 31 March 13. Panzer-Division had only 3 tanks (1 operational) and 8 anti-tank guns; its overall mobility had dropped to a mere 30%.[5] 11. Panzer-Division fared no better: it had 6 tanks (4 operational), 1 anti-tank gun and 4 artillery pieces.[6]

On 25 March 1944 the spearheads of 2nd Ukrainian Front reached the Prut, which partially formed the prewar border with Rumania. During the night of 25/26 March they crossed the river, thus becoming the first Soviet formation that brought the war to the enemy's territory.

Konev's offensive was spearheaded by strong forces: three tank armies and several independent cavalry and mechanized corps. Only two things could stop them from driving deep into Rumania: the muddy season and the Luftwaffe.

The mud was indeed a problem. Nearly all Soviet vehicles, even some tanks, bogged down. 6th Tank Army, for instance, was forced to stop for couple of days, because its supply lines were overstretched, the combat units had ran out of ammunition and there were not enough bridges over the Dniester and the Prut.[7]

The hardships of the 1944 spring campaign in the Ukraine were vividly recalled by one of army's most prominent warriors, Dmitriy Loza, who commanded some Sherman tanks of 5th Mechanized Corps:

> Conditions for the actions of the troops were exceptionally difficult. The rivers were running full and the roads and fields were a sea of mud. Only tracked vehicles could move, and the wheeled vehicles remained in assembly areas. In units of the 5th Mechanized Corps, Sherman tanks were used almost like draft animals. Fuel cells were mounted on their armor, along with boxes of shells and ammunition, and desantniki [tank riders].[…]

The Umansk-Botoshansk offensive operation was conducted in the most difficult conditions of the spring thaw. The thickness of the sticky layer of chernozem reached almost forty to fifty centimeters [fifteen to eighteen inches] on all the roads. After a nineteen-day offensive, units of the 5th Mechanized Corps seized the important crossroads at Vapnyarka [250 kilometers southwest of Kiev] on 15 March. This opened the way for a strong push to the south, toward the Dniester River. Only tanks could take full advantage of this opportunity. An assault group of four to five submachine gunners headed by a sergeant, and sometimes an officer, was placed on the Shermans and self-propelled guns in all the corps' brigades. Each combat vehicle also carried two or three crates of ammunition and one or two diesel fuel drums. This not insignificant load sharply reduced the maneuverability of the tanks and self-propelled guns. In the weather situation that had developed, there was no alternative. The wheeled supply columns would remain in the Vapnyarka area until the roads dried out.[8]

Alexander Rogachev, an anti-tank battery commander with the same corps, tells a similar story:

> Then we resumed the offensive. The spring muddy season was so bad that we couldn't keep up with our own infantry in our Willys jeeps. There was a sea in every low-lying area. We would get the guns across them by hitching them to tanks, while we would stand on the gun trails. We dragged the Willys jeeps across the same way. As a result, the infantry took seats on the tanks and Studebakers, while we were ordered to stop until the roads dried out.[9]

* * *

Throughout most of the Uman offensive the Luftwaffe was nowhere to be seen. The Axis planes were grounded by bad weather, let alone that they had to be moved to Rumanian bases. But once they relocated to northeast Rumania, where they could operate from hard-surface airfields and where they were well-supplied with fuel and ammunition, they struck again.

4    C. Duffy, "Red storm on the Reich", New York, Da Capo Press, 1993, p. 11.

5    Bundesarchiv-Militärarchiv, Freiburg, RH 10/151. (Hereafter BA-MA RH 10/151.)

6    BA-MA RH 10/149.

7    TsAMO, fu. 3443, inv. 1, f. 36, p. 96.

8    D. Loza, "Commanding the Red Army's Sherman Tanks", Lincoln, The University of Nebraska Press, 1996.

9    A. Drabkin (Ed.), "Ya dralsya s Panzerwaffe", Moscow, Yauza-Eksmo, 2007, p. 337.

The dangerous penetration of the Red Army spearheads into the northeastern borderlands of Rumania allowed the Axis pilots to show their true qualities. Often flying in large groups (40, 60 even 80 aircraft), the close-support planes of Air Fleet 4 bombed and strafed the advancing Soviets without mercy. They used smart and flexible tactics: the targets were attacked in waves, 5-6 minutes apart, the duration of each attack was typically short and repeatedly a method borrowed from the Soviets, the "circle of death", was employed.[10]

Unlike the previous campaigns, this time the German and Rumanian airmen paid very little attention to the ground communications of the Soviets and focused their attention almost exclusively on their forward lines.[11] Needless to say, Konev's tanks were among their favorite targets. Thus, from 26 to 29 March alone, in the Soroki - Fălești area (straight north of Iași) the Ju 87's, Fw 190's and Hs 129's destroyed 18 tanks.[12]

The men who flew those machines literally knew no rest, flying hundreds of sorties a day. Among them was the celebrated *Panzerknacker* Hans-Ulrich Rudel:

> The next morning our reconnaissance discovers strong armoured and motorized formations already almost due N. of Balti, probably they have even reached the town. At first the weather is bad; the country is mountainous and the highest peaks are shrouded in mist.
>
> The situation is grave; there are no longer any troops covering our front. Motorized units can get here in half a day. Who is to stop them? We stand alone. Reconnaissance reports strong opposition by flak, which the advancing Reds have brought up with them. Soviet Lag 5s and Airacobras continually fly above their armoured spearhead. Our southern front in Russia, the Rumanian oilfields, both factors of vital importance, are threatened. I am blind and deaf to all advice with regard to my physical condition. The Soviets must be checked; their tanks, the striking force of an army, destroyed. Another week goes by before our colleagues on the ground can build a defense line. [...]
>
> We attack tanks, supply convoys with petrol and rations, infantry and cavalry, with bombs and cannon. We attack from between 30 and 600 feet because the weather is execrable.

I go out with aircraft of my anti-tank flight carrying the 3.7cm. cannon on tank hunts at the lowest possible level. Soon all the rest of the flight are grounded because when my aircraft is hit I have to use another, and so one after the other gets a rest. If it takes too long to refuel the whole squadron. I have my aircraft and another quickly refueled and remunitioned, and the two of us go out between sorties on one of our own. Generally there are none of our fighters there; the Russians realize their enormous numerical superiority over us alone. Maneuvering is difficult in these air battles, for I am unable to operate the rudder controls, I only use the stick. But up till now I have only been hit by flak; in every sortie, however, and that is often enough. [...] I drop down below the squadron and fly low over the village, and am met by flak and strong opposition. I see a mass of tanks, behind them a long convoy of lorries and motorized infantry. The tanks are, curiously, all carrying two or three drums of petrol. In a flash it dawns upon me; they no longer expected us and mean to dash through tonight, if possible into the heart of Rumania, into the oil region, and thereby cutting off our southern front. They are taking advantage of the twilight and the darkness because by day they cannot move with my Stukas overhead. This also accounts for the petrol drums on board the tanks; they mean, if necessary, to push through even without their supply columns. This is a major operation and they are already under way. I now see that perfectly plainly. We are alone to possess this knowledge; the responsibility is ours. [...]

Each time I come in to the attack I am sensible of the responsibility which rests on us and hope we may be successful. What luck that we spotted this convoy today! I have run out of ammunition; have just knocked out five tanks but there are still a few monsters in the fields, some of them even yet moving. I long to put paid to them somehow. [...]

Explosions briefly illuminate the battle field with an eerie light. Visibility is now pretty poor. I head north, flying at low level along the road and catch up with two steel monsters travelling in the same direction, probably with the intention of carrying the sad news back to the rear. I bank and am on to them; I can only discern them at the very last second as I skim the ground. They are not an easy target, but as they, like their predecessors, carry the big drums, I succeed in blowing them both up, though I have to use up all my ammunition. With these two, a total of seventeen tanks for the day. My squadron has destroyed approximately the same number, so that today the Ivans have lost some thirty tanks. A rather black day for the enemy. Tonight at all events we can sleep quietly at Jassy [Iași],

10   TsAMO, fu. 240, inv. 2779, f. 879, p. 73.
11   Ibid.
12   TsAMO, fu. 240, inv. 2779, f. 879, p. 63.

of that we can be sure. How far the general impetus of the offensive has been impaired we shall learn tomorrow. We make our final landing in the dark. Now gradually I become conscious of pain, as the tension slowly relaxes. Both the army and the air group want to know every detail. For half the night I sit by the telephone with the receiver to my ear.

The mission for tomorrow is obvious: to engage the same enemy forces as today.[13]

On 29 March three divisions of 53rd Army, supported by tanks, anti-tank artillery and fighter aircraft, finally secured Balta, a major rail junction and one of the main German exit points from the Ukraine. It seemed that nothing could now stop Konev from driving into the heart of Rumania. But all of a sudden, his offensive began to lose momentum.

## MALINOVSKY STRIKES, TOO

Army-General Malinovsky launched his own offensive on 6 March, when his 3rd Ukrainian Front attacked along the Black Sea coast in the general direction of Odessa.

Vasily Grossman, a Soviet writer and journalist who was attached to the headquarters of 3rd Ukrainian Front as a war correspondent, colorfully described the outset of the operation in his private papers:

Before the attack, the Military Council of the Front had been thinking above all of the weather. They kept looking at the barometer. A professor of meteorology had been summoned, as well as an old man, expert in the local weather, who could forecast it by looking at some indications of which no one else knew. Officers attended lectures on meteorology.

On 6 March, General Rodion I. Malinovsky's 3rd Ukrainian Front launched an offensive along the Black Sea coast to capture Odessa. The enemy consisted of the German Sixth Army, a recreation of the original army at Stalingrad – this was on Hitler's orders, as if it would wipe out the defeat. [...]

Advancing in the mud requires an enormous physical effort. Quantities of petrol which would otherwise have been sufficient to go hundreds of kilometers are

burned up over a few hundred meters. Mobile groups are cutting off German communications, supplies and liaison. Sometimes Germans retreat chaotically. The whole steppe is filled with the howling of vehicles and tractors tearing themselves out of the mud. The 'roads' are hundreds of meters wide.[14]

*Troops of 3rd Ukrainian Front deal with the deep mud in the vicinity of Krivoi Rog, March1944. (Olga Lander collection)*

The offensive was spearheaded by the cavalry-mechanized group of Lieutenant-General Pliev that consisted of a cavalry corps and a mechanized corps.[15] Being a very experienced cavalry officer, Pliev knew how to conduct a raid deep in the enemy's rear and already by the third day of the battle most of the German 6. Army was encircled southwest of Krivoi Rog. Thus, the Red cavalry once again proved its value, because it was forced to operate in terrain that bore no difference to the rest of the Ukraine (that's to say, it was a sea of mud). But the operational success came at the cost of heavy losses: by 18 March the group was down to just 11 tanks (out of 106) and had lost 1,257 men in killed and wounded. 20 of its tanks had become total write-offs, many other had been knocked out or had been abandoned due to mechanical breakdowns.[16]

9

13  H.-U. Rudel, "Stuka Pilot", New York, Bantam Books, 1984.

14  V. Grossman, "A Writer at War", London, The Harvill Press, 2005.
15  4th Guards Cavalry Corps and 4th Guards Mechanized Corps.
16  TsAMO, fu. 243, inv. 2900, f. 156, p. 59.

*General-Lieutenant Pliev at Odessa, first days of April 1944. (Olga Lander collection)*

The commander of 6. Army, Generaloberst Karl-Adolf Hollidt, was well aware what was in store for his men and immediately ordered a breakout to the west. Thus a "second Stalingrad" was avoided and most of the troops were saved, even though they were forced, like their neighbors to the north, to leave behind many of their heavy weapons and equipment.

## CLAIMS OF 3RD UKRAINIAN FRONT FOR 6-15 MARCH 1944

**Destroyed:**
- 30,700 troops
- 140 tanks
- 105 self-propelled guns
- 6,860 motor vehicles

**Captured:**
- 9,353 troops
- 131 tanks
- 174 self-propelled guns
- 671 artillery pieces
- 9,100 motor vehicles.[17]

The breakout effort of 6. Army to a considerable degree was facilitated by the fact that Hollidt had five armored divisions at his disposal, though none of them was at full strength. They detached some of their remaining operational AFVs and assembled them into small (4-7 panzers or/and assault-guns), but highly mobile armored battle groups. The latter were repeatedly employed in rearguard actions, mostly in local counterattacks, as well as to cover the retreat of the main forces by firing on the approaching Soviets from well-concealed positions.[18] One such action was vividly told by Josef Allerberger, the sniper ace of 3. Mountain Division:

It was in low spirits that our motley unit plodded towards the bridgehead alongside columns of 3.G.D. vehicles. The size of the evacuation lent a feeling

17    TsAMO, fu. 243, inv. 2900, f. 1149, p. 4.
18    TsAMO, fu. 243, inv. 2900, f. 1149, p. 9.

of security. At the approach to the Ingulez [River], I saw through intense hail the two regimental commanders in discussion with their staffs about how to defend the crossing point. I was approaching to report my presence when, while still about 30 meters away, there came a warning shout: 'Achtung! Ivan! Tank!' At that moment a T-34 became dimly visible and opened fire with its MGs. A horse was hit and began to whinny pitifully while our troops dispersed and sprinted for cover. An SP-gun attempted to maneuver into position to return fire. […] Some of the regimental staff officers had thrown themselves to the ground as the tank turret swiveled to take them under fire. Flames leapt from the muzzle of the beast's main gun and the shell, narrowly missing the prostrate officers, turned a group of vehicles into a heap of twisted and burning metal. […] The German SP-gun fired at the tank and hit the turret. There was a dull explosion and the T-34 burst into flame. The occupants were probably fried, for they made no attempt to escape. Within minutes the danger had passed.[19]

Hollidt's decision to break out of the cauldron before it was fully closed by the Soviet infantry was not only timely, but also proved to be a game-changing one. The panzer divisions were immediately pulled out of action, loaded on trains and urgently transferred to the Iaşi area in northeast Rumania, where they arrived just in time to prevent the Soviets from breaking into the hinterland. Thus, 8. Army was provided with readily available reserves (three panzer-divisions) exactly when they were needed most.

Here is the place to say that during the fighting withdrawal from the southern Ukraine the panzer-divisions in question had managed to spare most of their men. However, this was achieved only at the expense of abandoning most their armored and soft-skinned vehicles, as well as a considerable part of their guns. (On 31 March, for instance, 23. Panzer-Division did not have even a single tank or assault gun.[20]) Worse still, most of its personnel were totally exhausted and demoralized. One of those men was Armin Böttger, a panzer radio operator with 24. Panzer-Division:

Back to our departure from the unbattleworthy 1244 [Pz IV tank]. With great difficulty we made our way along the congested main highway, first on foot and then hitchhiking, to a front command post at Pervomaysk on the Bug river. From there we were sent to Odessa by train. It was absolutely packed and we stood the whole 54 hours. I had seen German troops retreating often enough and looking at the Bug I wondered why at least some kind of expanded defensive line had not been set up along this wide river, if not a kind of Westwall. German troops had fought outstandingly in numerous bloody defensive battles, but they still kept on pulling back.

On 19 March 1944 the rest of the 1244 crew joined us at Odessa. Up to this point, as far as I know, my division and regiment had always seized the initiative and held its ground in all previous actions. I had always gone forward with 24.Pzr. Regt. Now one saw only too clearly that we were going back and only back. For the first time I was fleeing, and this was a demoralizing realization.

Depressed, I described in a letter to my mother that although I was a soldier with an especially strong division, I had been to a certain extent pulling back for a few days. Now even I doubted in victory, as had my mother always.[21]

* * *

Upon the retreat of 6. Army beyond the southern Bug, the frontline temporary stabilized along the western bank. Until 28 March Hollidt's badly mauled divisions managed to contain Malinovsky's seven armies. The latter, in turn, were not in a hurry to surge forward again, because they were busy enlarging their vital bridgeheads on the western bank of the river, as well as resupplying their combat units.[22]

Vasily Grossman described the advance of 3rd Ukrainian Front in a very lively manner for an article published in the Krasnaya Zvezda newspaper:

Finally, the sun is getting hotter and hotter, and light clouds of dust have already appeared flying behind the trucks. A thin, swarthy captain in a greatcoat whose flaps are covered with scales of brown and red earth inhaled this dust with delight: 'Oh, imagine how dreadful the mud has been if dust – this scourge of the war – now seems nicer than all the spring flowers. For us, the dust smells good today. 'Several days ago, a shrill howling of one-and-a-half-ton trucks, three-tonners, five-ton YAZ tractors, caterpillar transporters, Dodges and Studebakers hung constantly over this steppe. They were howling in an angry effort to break out

19  A. Wacker, "Sniper on the Eastern Front", Barnsley, Pen & Sword, 2005.
20  BA-MA RH 10/160.

21  A. Böttger, "To the Gate of Hell", Barnsley, Frontline Books, 2012.
22  TsAMO, fu. 243, inv. 2900, f. 1149, p. 4.

from the mud's claws to catch up with the sleepless infantry. Their fierce but powerless wheels only threw out sticky lumps of mud, spinning in the oily, slippery ruts. And thousands of sinewy, thin, sweating people were heaving at the rear ends [of bogged-down vehicles], their teeth clenched, day and night, under the eternal rain and the eternal, three times accursed, wet, melting snow... Who will recount the great feats of our people? Who will recreate the epic of this unprecedented offensive, this sleepless advance that went on day and night? Infantrymen were marching, loaded with one and a half issues of ammunition, and their greatcoats wet and as heavy as lead. A severe north wind sprang upon them, their greatcoats froze and became rigid like sheet iron. Cushions of mud, weighing a pound apiece, stuck to the boots. Sometimes, people only managed a kilometer an hour, so hard was this road. For many kilometers around, there wasn't a dry patch of land. Soldiers had to sit down in the mud to have some rest or take off their boots to rewrap their foot cloths. Mortar men were moving forward beside the riflemen, and each of them was carrying half a dozen bombs hanging on loops of rope on their backs and chests. ' That's all right,' they said. 'It's even harder for the Germans. It's death for Germans now...'

No work was more terrible than building a bridge over the southern Bug. The sappers only had a tiny bridgehead on the west bank, the enemy was pressing hard, and the sappers were building the bridge not just under German fire, but right in the midst of the firing itself. The marsh seemed bottomless: a test pile went in eleven meters deep, as if into pastry.[23]

Malinovsky resumed his offensive on 27 March. By then the left wing of the neighboring 2nd Ukrainian Front had penetrated the Axis defense at Pervomaysk, crossing the southern Bug in the process. That success was immediately exploited by the right flank of 3rd Ukrainian Front where Malinovsky had assembled a strong task force (37th and 57th Armies, Pliev's group and 23rd Tank Corps). The powerful

---

23  Grossman, op. cit.

*Two Soviet 76-mm regimental guns support the attacking infantry of one of the divisions of 3rd Ukrainian Front at Tiraspol, first days of April 1944. (Olga Lander collection)*

12

blow delivered by the adjacent flanks of both Fronts quickly fragmented the German position and effectively separated Hollidt's 6. Army from its left-hand neighbor, 8. Army of General Wöhler. By the end of 28 March there was a 25-km-wide gap between the two German armies and Malinovsky pushed through it his main mobile forces, Pliev's group and 23rd Tank Corps. He directed them to the southwest, toward Tiraspol and Razdelnaya.[24]

## ORDER-OF-BATTLE AND STRENGTH OF THE MOBILE FORCES OF 3RD UKRAINIAN FRONT, 28 MARCH 1944

**Order of battle:**
- 23rd Tank Corps
- 4th Guards Mechanized Corps
- 4th Guards Cavalry Corps
- Three independent tank regiments
- Six independent self-propelled artillery regiments

**AFV strength:**
- 265 tanks
- 98 self-propelled guns[25]

As usual, the Red tankers and cavalrymen raised hell in the Axis rear zone. They did not operate in large formations, but in combat teams spearheaded by scouting detachments. Josef Allerberger recalls one of his encounters with the Red mechanized scouts:

The two days' forced march failed to bring about the hoped-for respite: the Russians maintained their stranglehold on the division and the retreat soon degenerated into an ugly free-for-all without well-drawn battle lines. The Soviets were everywhere, creating islands of German resistance that had no option but to fight on alone in the hope of regaining contact later with the main group. The Russian infantry had a new battlefield vehicle; armoured half-tracks for infantry transport supplied under the terms of the US Lend-Lease Pact. These machines were obviously very useful for getting Russian soldiers into and behind

*Infantrymen of 3rd Ukrainian Front attack along a destroyed German armored train (Panzerzug 70) at the Razdelnaya train station, first days of April 1944. (Olga Lander collection)*

our lines, where they would disembark and immediately start fighting. The danger could be averted with anti-tank guns, but we had nothing more powerful than hand-grenades to do the job.[26]

The only way to stop the powerful Soviet armored wedges, as usual, was to call in the Luftwaffe. The appearance of the tank-killing planes, be they German Ju 87 or Rumanian Hs 129, was always welcomed by the Axis ground troops. Allerberger continues his story:

To our astonishment, OKH sent to our aid a number of Rumanian bomber aircraft and an anti-tank detachment. They destroyed twenty-four Russian tanks and gave us the breathing space needed to construct a new defensive line. After fighting for months without air support, the sight of friendly aircraft seemed almost surreal.[27]

**13**

24   "Istoria na Vtorata Svetovna Voina 1939 - 1945", Vol. 8, Sofia, Voenno izdatelstvo, 1980, pp. 108-109.
25   TsAMO, fu. 243, inv. 2900, f. 728, p. 5.
26   Wacker, op. cit.
27   Ibid.

Indeed, the Axis pilots inflicted very heavy losses on the rapidly advancing Soviet mobile formations. Thus, on 31 March 1944 alone Pliev's group lost in the vicinity of Novotroitskoe (some 140 km north of Odessa) 39 tanks due to aerial attacks.[28] On the same day Pliev's main armored component, 4th Guards Mechanized Corps, was hit hard at Berezovka (about 70 km to the southeast of Novotroitskoe) by several groups of close-support Axis planes ranging from 8 to 23 aircraft. The corps lost 108 men in killed and wounded, as well as two tanks and eight motor vehicles. On the afternoon of the next day the Luftwaffe struck again, this time with about 50 aircraft. As result of that, 4th Guards Mechanized Corps was crippled, losing 19 tanks destroyed and two more temporarily put out of action.[29]

*M-72 motorcycles and T-34 tanks of 4th Guards Mechanized Corps in the vicinity of Odessa, spring 1944. (Olga Lander collection)*

Even though Air Fleet 4 had several types of close-support aircraft, the experts of the command staff of the armored troops of 3rd Ukrainian Front were particularly impressed by the combat qualities of the latest German fighter-bomber, the Fw 190. In their after-action report they pointed out that its on-board 2 cm cannons were capable of penetrating heavy AFVs like ISU-152 from one side to the other. Some of the tanks inspected by them had been penetrated by 8-10 such rounds.[30]

**LOSSES OF THE MOBILE FORCES OF 3RD UKRAINIAN FRONT, 28 MARCH – 14 APRIL 1944**

- Personnel: 765 killed and 1,451 wounded
- Tanks: 102 destroyed and 48 knocked-out
- Self-propelled guns: 18 destroyed and 17 knocked-out
- Trucks: 41 destroyed
- Special-purpose motor vehicles: 5 destroyed
- Armored cars: 3 destroyed[31]

* * *

The murderous strafing attacks of the Luftwaffe didn't stop Pliev's men. They approached Razdelnaya, perhaps the biggest rail junction in the southwestern Ukraine, which was used by the Germans to evacuate the rest of 6. Army. This raid once again created panic in the Axis rear area and had grave consequences for many.

Among those who found themselves trapped at the Razdelnaya train station were some elements of SS-Panzer-Regiment 3 (3. SS-Panzer-Division *"Totenkopf"*). On 2 April 1944 the transport carrying seven Tigers from regiment's 9. company was brought to a halt at the station along with thirty other rail transports. It turned out that Russians (Pliev's cavalry-mechanized group) had cut off the retreat routes. Before long a German Army staff officer approached the company commander and ordered him to blow up the remaining tanks as the enemy was not far away. Eric Lehmkuhl recalls this event:

> The remnants of the tank regiment were loaded on rail transports heading in the direction of Tiraspol when we came to a standstill along with thirty other rail transports. Because of the Russian rapid advance, we are ordered to blow up our remaining Tigers. We had hoped that our transport carrying the Tigers would have been given priority and forwarded onto Tiraspol. The crews had to provide themselves with supplies, which were gathered from other transports. We have to make our way westward on foot, but to add insult to injury, we

28    TsAMO, fu. 243, inv. 2900, f. 728, p. 7.
29    TsAMO, fu. 3344, inv. 1, f. 21, p. 256.
30    TsAMO, fu. 307, inv. 4148, f. 186, p. 141.

31    TsAMO, fu. 243, inv. 2900, f. 728, p. 10.

are hit by a snow storm, so we have to sit down with packs, ammunition, and weapons. Slowly, the storm rolls westward. As we move along, we notice many vehicles stuck in the mud. Some of these have to be blown up with hand grenades so the Russians cannot use them, but unfortunately, the crews have to get rid of certain items and carry the barest minimum. The crews always try to hitch a ride, but this rarely happens as operational vehicles are scarce.

At night we sleep in barns or haystacks, but we are always in fear of the advancing Russians. The next day, the column is scattered by a small group of Russian tanks. We reply with machine-gun fire. We manage to reach Tiraspol, where large groups of soldiers are gathered by the military police. These soldiers are formed into alarm groups for use in infantry *Kampfgruppen*. We are lucky — the field police let us by and pass through, and we find that *9. Kompanie* had set up a reporting center for the company's soldiers. The soldiers are assembled and transported by rail from Tiraspol to Kishinev (Chisinau), and from there we are transported to Bacau. I later found out that SS-Mann Werner from the *Instand-Staffel* was given fourteen days of hard labor for trying to sell his pistol for some rations.[32]

Razdelnaya was taken on 4 April. Immediately afterwards Pliev's tanks and cavalry swung to the southeast, towards Odessa. Now only a narrow corridor along the seacoast was left open for the retreat of the fleeing Germans and Rumanians. On 7 April it was shut down, too, when Pliev's mounted Cossacks reached the Dniester Estuary.

## TROPHIES AND PRISONERS CAPTURED BY PLIEV'S GROUP AT RAZDELNAYA, 6-7 APRIL 1944

- 3,000 troops (including many wounded in a hospital train)
- 40 tanks
- 5 self-propelled guns
- 180 artillery pieces
- 1,000 horse-drawn carts[33]

---

32    I. M. Wood, "Tigers of the Death's Head", Mechanicsburg, Stackpole Books, 2013.
33    TsAMO, fu. 243, inv. 2900, f. 729, p. 23.

No German of the "new" 6. Army wanted to suffer the fate of Paulus' old one at Stalingrad. Even though some surrendered or were captured, most of the troops kept moving forward. Josef Allerberger lively describes those days of panic and anxiety:

The pocket was 8 kilometers long by 4 broad; Bakalov [Bakalovo] town was along the western perimeter, the highest topographical point being 140 meters. The German units were in a desperate plight, battalions being composed of half-strength companies armed only with light infantry weapons and grenades. The men were starving and in poor physical condition, but the fear of falling into Russian hands had concentrated their minds powerfully. Wittmann, commanding general 3.G.D. was in overall command, his immediate priority being to break out of the encirclement and reach the German lines along the west bank of the Kutschurgan [River]. Besides the failure of logistics, the communications network had collapsed and messages were being passed by runners, wasting valuable hours that should have been devoted to planning the break-out strategy. […]

At first light on 6 April 1944, Gruppe Lorch attacked the encirclement at the northern perimeter below the 140-metre spot height, all reserves being called upon in the desperate struggle to escape. The official records speak of an heroic action planned and executed to the last detail, but the reality was organized chaos blessed with good fortune. Many men lost their nerve and fled in panic beforehand. Shortly before the decisive attack I was queuing at the last field kitchen to fill my tea-flask when through the swathes of morning mist there came the sound of roaring motors and squeaking tracks. Everybody stared towards the noise, straining to make out the tanks. There was still nothing to see when an hysterical voice yelled, 'It's Ivan! He's here! Tanks!' Most of the Jäger broke and ran. The catering sergeant mounted his horse in a flying leap and whipped the animal into a gallop, tea from the open containers aboard the wheeled field kitchen slopping in all directions. A few of the veterans tried to halt the panic. A few cuffs to the ear and kicks to the rear brought some of the men to their senses, but more than half had disappeared into the mist behind the field kitchen. The remainder waited for the death-dealing T-34s to materialize through the fog, and a few minutes later the German SP-guns, which had been sent up unannounced in support of the break-out, made their appearance. It was another half hour before the last of the fleeing made their

*Destroyed Axis vehicles in Odessa, April 1944.*
*(Author's collection)*

*Abandoned German Pz IV Ausf. J tanks in the Ukrainian town of Chernivtsi, April 1944. (RGAKFD)*

sheepish return, and accepted a kick in the pants as a disciplinary measure for their action.[34]

Terrified by the prospects of another Stalingrad, the Germans and Rumanians simply fled from the Odessa area. Unlike they previous cauldron battles, this time they even didn't try to conduct any significant rearguard actions. The main reason for that was perhaps the fact that by then they already had lost nearly all of their assault guns, with which they had used to slow down the Soviets. In those rare occasions when such actions were carried out, they were surprisingly successful, because the terrain favored the defenders.[35]

On 10 April the forces of two Soviet armies – 5th Shock- and 6th – captured Odessa by swift attack. Vasily Grossman entered the city with the liberators. Later on he wrote the following in his private papers:

> The day of the capture of Odessa. The port [is] empty. Puffs of smoke. Thunder of military vehicles and equipment pouring into the city. Crowds of people. Scorched corpses carried out of the Gestapo building. The charred corpse of a girl, with beautiful golden hair intact.[36]

In the meantime, those troops of 6. Army that had been trapped west and northwest of Odessa were completing their withdrawal. Even though the pursuing Soviets took 10,632 of them prisoner,[37] the bulk of three army corps[38] (with ten German and two Rumanian divisions), save for nearly all their heavy weapons and equipment, managed to extract themselves from the cauldron. One of those who found safety beyond the Dniester was Josef Allerberger:

> We kept on going for three more days, crossing the Dniester on 10 April. It was a portentous moment, the end of Barbarossa, for we had passed beyond the territorial limits of the Soviet Union and entered Rumanian Bessarabia. After three years of the most bitter fighting and horrendous losses, all now knew beyond the slightest doubt that the war was being brought ever closer to the Reich. The

---

34 Wacker, op. cit.
35 TsAMO, fu. 243, inv. 2900, f. 729, p. 59.
36 Grossman, op. cit.
37 TsAMO, fu. 243, inv. 2900, f. 729, p. 60.
38 XXIX., XXXXIV. and LXXII. Army Corps.

---

enemy we faced on this front had to be held, forever if possible. A tiny spark of hope still glimmered that somewhere, somehow, we could stop him permanently.[39]

**TROPHIES CAPTURED BY 3RD UKRAINIAN FRONT DURING THE BATTLE OF ODESSA**

- 207 locomotives
- 3,957 loaded boxcars
- 8,080 motor vehicles (mostly non-operational)
- 169 tanks
- 10 armored halftracks
- 223 artillery pieces
- 233 mortars
- 171 tractors and prime movers
- 31 ammunition dumps
- 21 food stores[40]

# THE FAILURE OF THE SOVIET SPRING OFFENSIVE IN RUMANIA

By the beginning of April 1944 the Soviet grandiose offensive in the Ukraine that had begun in the previous summer finally began to lose momentum. The German Army Group "South Ukraine", now under new commander (*Generaloberst* Schörner) and heavily reinforced with Rumanian divisions, at last was able to form a continuous frontline stretching from the Eastern Carpathians to the Black Sea. Following the disastrous retreat of the Axis troops from the Odessa area, its lower section was now running strictly along the western bank of the Dniester.

Schörner took over a totally exhausted and decimated force that was holding out with its last remaining strength against Konev's and Malinovsky's attacks. For political reasons (to calm down the reluctant ally) the army group was divided into

---

39 Wacker, op. cit.
40 TsAMO, fu. 243, inv. 2900, f. 729, p. 35.

Generaloberst Ferdinand Schörner meets Marshal Ion Antonescu on an airfield in Rumania, May 1944. (NAC)

General der Infanterie Otto Wöhler, the Commander-in-Chief of Armeegruppe Wöhler. (NARA)

General der Artillerie Maximilian de Angelis, the commander of 6. Army (April – July 1944). In July 1944 he was appointed commander of 2. Panzer-Army, which operated in Central Yugoslavia. (NARA)

General Petru Dumitrescu, the only Rumanian holder of the Knight's Cross with oak Leaves. From April to August 1944 he was in command of Armeegruppe Dumitrescu, a provisional army detachment made of the Rumanian 3. Army and the German 6. Army. (NAC)

two clearly distinguishable parts. The Iaşi sector was assigned to the German-led *Armeegruppe Wöhler* (Army Detachment "Wöhler"), while the Dniester front became the responsibility of the Rumanian-led *Armeegruppe Dumitrescu*. The former was made of Wöhler's 8. Army and the Rumanian 4. Army, while the latter – of the Rumanian 3. Army of General Dumitrescu and the German 6. Army, which now operated under a new commander, the Austrian-born highly decorated veteran of the Eastern Front *General der Artillerie* Maximilian de Angelis. (Hollidt was sacked by the beginning of April 1944.)

By mid-April 1944 Army Group "South Ukraine" consisted of more than 40 German and 23 Rumanian divisions, but some of them were in such a sorry state that they existed only on paper. Not surprisingly, the first task of the army group's new commander-in-chief was therefore to replenish the battle-worn formations as quickly as possible, secure their supply lines and strengthen the main line of resistance.

Even though the weapons and supplies began to arrive in growing quantities and the staying power of the frontline troops gradually improved, one problem remained unsolved – no one in the German camp had much confidence in the fighting strength of the Rumanian troops. Even Hitler himself was infected by pessimism – on 2 April he ordered that Rumanian divisions be deployed only in such a way that front sections liable to attack by Soviet armor were defended exclusively by German units.

The ordinary German combatants were also not impressed by the overall fighting quality of their Rumanian allies. The pompous award ceremonies, the joint drills, the extensive training given by German instructors to the Rumanian units and the sporadic delivery of modern weapons could do very little in this regard.

One of the many Germans that were generally dissatisfied by the Rumanian "brothers in arms" was the young *Leutnant* von Eggeling, who in the spring of 1944 was detached with some Panthers of 11. Panzer-Division to support a Rumanian division, giving "these poor folks the illusion of infinite strength":

> My weeks with the Rumanian division was a nightmare all the time. The officers were drunk and had the best food class 1, the sergeants had class 2, and the common soldiers nothing more than 'mammaliga,' which is a mush of maize. They had even no leather boots but rags over their feet. You can imagine how the fighting spirit was.[41]

But the distrust went both ways, not least because the Nazi officials and senior officers seldom were able to provide what they had promised, many of the German soldiers behaved arrogantly, let alone that the country had become a permanent target of the Allied bombing raids and mainly because everyone was well aware who was going to win the war.

* * *

Konev's ultimate victory in the Ukraine came at a cost – in March 1944 his 2nd Ukrainian Front had lost about 56,800 men (including ca. 11,500 killed).[42] Those losses were quickly made good, because during the same month some 108,000 were drafted in the liberated areas to take the place of the fallen.[43]

The replacements that were continually coming from the rear zones, however, caused very little enthusiasm among the seasoned veterans. The latter, however, were well aware that the forcibly conscripted Ukrainians would be no match for the experienced combatants lost in the last battles. Among them was Vladimir Zimakov, an anti-tank rifleman with 202nd Rifle Division (27th Army), who recalls his first impression of the unfortunate draftees:

Well, approximately a week went by, and we received a small batch of replacements from the local population – men born in 1926 and 1927. They were all rounded up and sent to the front. We called them 'Blackshirts', because they were all wearing dark shirts, as well as grey coats. They hadn't been given uniforms.[44]

Marshal Konev, however, had no control over two very decisive factors: the weather and the terrain. It was these two factors that contributed to a certain degree to the failure of the Soviet spring offensive in Rumania.

* * *

In the evening of 5 April the Stavka (the Soviet Supreme Command) ordered 2nd Ukrainian Front to advance further into Rumania and capture Botoşani and Iaşi.[45] Stalin was well aware that Konev would need reinforcements, that's why he already had dispatched the full-strength 3rd Guards Tank Corps (with nearly 300 tanks and self-propelled guns, including some factory-fresh T-34/85).

Konev intended to form a powerful "shock" group on his right flank comprising 40th, 27th and 52nd Armies, plus 5th Guards and 2nd Tank Armies, with which to crush the Axis defense in the Botoşani - Iaşi area. Iaşi itself was to be taken already on 7 April. It was to be used as a jump-off point for both tank armies. They were to be committed to battle on 9-10 April and wasting no time to advance toward Târgu Frumos and Roman, taking both towns from the march.[46]

It was a good plan, but this time the luck betrayed him. The flooded rivers, the mud and the spring thaw considerably delayed the redeployment of both tank armies. Instead of being unleashed en masse, 2nd Tank Army and 5th Guards Tank Army were thrown into action piecemeal on 12 and 15 April respectively.[47] Worse still, by then the Germans already had closed the gap in their frontline, by delivering a powerful counterattack into the left flank of the Soviet wedge with two of the armored divisions hurriedly transferred from 6. Army (24. Panzer- and *"Grossdeutschland"*). But this was not all. On 15 April General Wöhler struck again with these two crack divisions and expelled the Russians from Târgu Frumos.

41    A. Harding Ganz, "Ghost Division", Mechanicsburg, Stackpole Books, 2016, p. 228.
42    Wacker, op. cit.
43    TsAMO, fu. 240, inv. 2779, f. 879, p. 200.

44    A. Drabkin (Ed.), "Ya dralsya s Panzerwaffe", Moscow, Yauza-Eksmo, 2007, p. 337.
45    *Stavka* directives # 220072 and # 220073. TsAMO, fu. 148a, inv. 3763, f. 166, pp. 78-80. Reproduced in V. Zolotarev, "*Velikaia Otechestvennaia Voina*", Vol. 16(5-4), Terra, Moscow, 1999, pp. 71-72.
46    TsAMO, fu. 240, inv. 2779, f. 992, pp. 5-6.
47    TsAMO, fu. 240, inv. 2779, f. 992, p. 6.

*German troops in Iași after an exhausting fighting withdrawal from the Ukraine 1944; an RSO tractor in the background, ca. 10 April 1944. (Werner Geier)*

*Pz IV tank and panzer-grenadiers of Division "Grossdeutschland" prepare for counterattack, Iași area, May/June 1944. (Author's collection)*

*Officers and men of Panzer-Grenadier-Division "Grossdeutschland" have a rest near a Panzer-befehlswagen Panther Ausf. A command tank, Iași area, May/June 1944. (Author's collection)*

*General Hasso von Manteuffel, the commander of Panzer-Grenadier-Division "Grossdeutschland", inspects a forward position in the vicinity of Iași, May/June 1944. (NAC)*

Konev didn't give up and decided to further reinforce his "shock" group by shifting his 7th Guards Army from his left flank to the Târgu Frumos area. But Wöhler forestalled him again. On 25 April his panzer task force surprisingly struck the positions of the newly arrived 7th Guards Army north of Târgu Frumos and pushed the Russians back, capturing several villages in the process. Thus, Konev was deprived of a key jump-off point. The Soviet "shock" group, in turn, went over to the offensive on the next day with the objective of enveloping the Axis forces holding the Kishinev "bulge", but the moment of surprise had been lost and the armies failed to make an inroad.

The series of setbacks didn't discourage Stalin. He insisted an all out assault to be launched in early May, which objective was no less than knocking Rumania out of the war. Konev was ordered to breach the Axis positions west of Iaşi, then swiftly to advance toward Bucharest, which had to be taken from the march, eventually occupying the Ploesti oilfields during the final stage of the operation. [48] Apart from that, the "shock" group of 2nd Ukrainian Front had to swing part of its forces to the southeast, thereby encircling the German and Rumanian divisions of *Armeegruppe Dumitrescu* in the vicinity of Kishinev. Apparently, this plan was out of touch with the reality of the situation, but Stalin's ambitions knew no limits and Konev hadn't any other choice but to obey.

The attack was to be launched on a broad front between Suceava and Iaşi by four all-arms armies (40th, 7th Guards, 27th and 52nd) and three tank armies (2nd, 5th Guards and 6th). The main blow was to be delivered in the vicinity of Târgu Frumos by the bulk of 7th Guards and 27th Armies in close cooperation with 5th Guards and 2nd Tank Armies. Big hopes were placed on the super-strong 3rd Guards Tank Corps that had just assembled in the main jump-off area. It was assigned to Marshal Rotmistrov's 5th Guards Tank Army. Apart from that, both tank armies were reinforced with regiments outfitted with latest models Soviet heavy AFVs, namely IS-2 tanks and ISU-152 self-propelled guns.

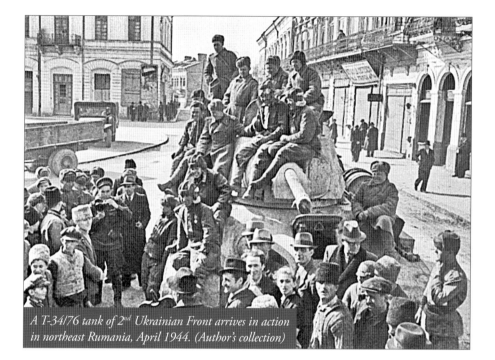

A T-34/76 tank of 2nd Ukrainian Front arrives in action in northeast Rumania, April 1944. (Author's collection)

**STRENGTH OF THE SOVIET TANK ARMIES IN THE TÂRGU FRUMOS, 1 MAY 1944**

2nd **Tank Army (Colonel-General Semyon Bogdanov):**
82 T-34, 5 IS-85, 19 IS-2, 3 Mk IX, 5 SU-85 =
133 tanks and self-propelled guns
5th **Guards Tank Army (Marshal of the Armored Troops Pavel Rotmistrov):**
183 T-34, 13 IS-2, 33 Mk IX, 42 M4 A2, 21 SU-76M, 22 SU-85, 18 ISU-152, 26 SU-57 (T48 halftrack) = 358 tanks and self-propelled guns[49]

Part of the AFVs of both tank armies were detached for close-support duty. This was perhaps a correct decision, because the Soviet rifle divisions didn't have any organic tanks or self-propelled guns and their assault teams had to deal with a dense web of field fortifications. Otherwise, the offensive was very poorly prepared. Many of the recently drafted Ukrainians were inadequately trained, the cooperation between the various branches (especially between the tanks and the infantry) was almost non existent. Worse still, the solid "Trajan" Line, a permanent defensive position stretching from the Carpathian slopes to Iaşi that consisted of many concrete bunkers, was insufficiently reconnoitered. (The senior officers of 7th Guards Army, for instance, even didn't know that their troops were going to deal with bunkers.) [50]

The Soviet offensive began in the early hours of 2 May. It was preceded by the usual hour-long preliminary artillery bombardment. Wöhler had anticipated the attack and withdrew their forces from the first lines of trenches just before the Red artillery would have pounded them. (The Soviet buildup was not a secret for the Axis intelligence and the probing attacks repelled on the previous day undoubtedly had

**23**

48   TsAMO, fu. 341, inv. 5312, f. 612, p. 4.
49   TsAMO, fu. 243, inv. 2900, f. 728, p. 5.

50   TsAMO, fu. 341, inv. 5312, f. 612, p. 3.

alerted Wöhler and his aides.) By nightfall Konev's "shock" group had advanced up to 10 km, capturing several villages in the process. Some of its forward detachments reached the outskirts of Tărgu Frumos, but were not able to advance any further.

*General der Panzertruppe Friedrich Kirchner (the commander of LVII. Panzer Corps) and General Radu Korne (the commander of the Rumanian 1. Armored Division) at a command post at Iași, May/June 1944. (NAC)*

It was the skilled leadership of LVII. Panzer Corps (*General der Panzertruppe Friedrich Kirchner*) and especially the brilliant performance of its two main formations (*"Grossdeutschland"* and 24. Panzer-Divisions) that brought to a halt Konev's offensive. They repeatedly counterattacked the Soviet wedges, inflicting heavy losses on both tank armies. The Axis artillery and the troops occupying the bunkers also stood fast. Even the appearance on the battlefield of the latest model Soviet tanks, namely T-34/85 and IS-2, didn't discourage the defenders. By the end of 5 May Konev's offensive clearly had shot its bolt. Not only the "shock" group had failed to break into open country, but the forces operating on both flanks (40th Army and the task force combining 6th Tank and 52nd Armies) also were pinned down. Stalin finally came to the realization that Rumania was not going surrender and already on the following day (6 May) ordered both 2nd and 3rd Ukrainian Fronts to go over to the defensive. [51]

*A soldier of Panzer-Grenadier-Division "Grossdeutschland" destroys a T-34 tank with a Panzerfaust in the vicinity of Iași, May/June 1944. (NAC).*

---

51   *Stavka* directives # 220094 and # 220095. TsAMO, fu. 148a, inv. 3763, f. 166, pp. 359-360. Reproduced in V. Zolotarev, *"Velikaia Otechestvennaia Voina"*, Vol. 16(5-4), Terra, Moscow, 1999, pp. 84-85.

*A German soldier inspects a destroyed IS-2 tank, Târgu Frumos, the beginning of May 1944. (Author's collection)*

\* \* \*

One of the main reasons for the failure of the Soviet spring offensive in northeastern Rumania in general, and in particular that at Târgu Frumos, was definitely the Axis superiority in the air. In its after-action report the operations section of 5th Guards Tank Army mentioned that the units had been hit hard by the Luftwaffe already on Day 1 (2 May) and that the friendly air force, save for a couple of patrolling fighters, was nowhere to be seen.

The tank-kill claims of the German and Rumanian pilots clearly show that they had many targets to choose from:

- 2 May 1944: 50 tanks
- 3 May 1944: 36 tanks and 3 self-propelled guns
- 4 May 1944: 10 tanks destroyed and 1 more knocked out
- 5 May 1944: 11 tanks destroyed and 11 other knocked out [52]

The devastating effect of the Axis aerial attacks is confirmed by several Soviet after-action reports, as well as by testimonies of many participants in the battle. One of them was Nikolai Shishkin, an ISU-152 commander with 1545th Guards Heavy Self-Propelled Regiment (5th Guards Tank Army):

There was another memorable incident that took place near Târgu-Frumos. I had summoned all the self-propelled gun commanders to my vehicle, in order to give them their orders. They took them and started to run off back to their vehicles, but one of them, Iura Krashennikov, delayed a bit. At this time a group of Ju-87s appeared and began to bomb us. The infantrymen who had been assigned to me scattered and dropped prone. Whenever a bomb was falling, I would watch to see where it would land, and then I would run and kick the prone men, so that they would move to the opposite side of the self-propelled gun, instead of lying there like logs. They would get sprayed with fragments, while I always managed to take shelter behind the vehicle. This time we were running from the bomb, and then we saw that it appeared as if it was going to drop right into the open hatch of the self-propelled gun commanded by Iura. Shocked by the realization that he'd been saved by a miracle by lingering next to my vehicle, he immediately went grey and began to stammer. I even had to send him to a hospital for treatment. [53]

Shishkin himself was also wounded later in the battle:

There was very hard fighting around Târgu-Frumos. In May 1944, I was wounded near this city. We were standing in one of the positions, ready to attack. The Germans were pounding us relentlessly with artillery fire, and then several dozen German aircraft appeared overhead just as I had popped my head out of the commander's hatch to take a look around. Just then an artillery shell or bomb exploded near the vehicle. I dropped back inside the fighting compartment and felt like I had banged a rib against the edge of the hatch. I felt a bit sick. I passed my hand over the spot that had taken the blow and looked – it was all bloody. A fragment had struck me in the back. I said aloud, 'Guys, I've been wounded.' They quickly patched me up and the regiment's assistant commander of the administrative unit took me to a hospital. [54]

52    Appendix to war diary of 8. Army. National Archives Records Administration Microfilm Series T312, roll 67, frames 7586827-7586870. (Hereafter cited as NARA T312/67/7586827-7586870.)

53    Drabkin, "Ya dralsya s Panzerwaffe", p. 239.
54    Ibid., p. 238.

Here is the place to say that the Soviet pilots did their best to support the friendly ground troops. During the four-day offensive they conducted a total of 1,967 combat sorties. But their opponents simply outperformed them. As the after-action analysis of 5th Air Army indicates, in the period in question the German and Rumanian pilots flew 5,107 sorties. Perhaps the main reason for this spectacular number was the closeness of the Axis airfields to the battlefield (8-12 km). The tactics employed by the combat units of Air Fleet 4 was also very effective. They appeared over the combat zone in waves. The fighters arrived first; they chased away their Soviet counterparts. Then the fighter-bombers and ground-attack planes (Fw 190 and Hs 129) strafed the Red ground units. After that the third wave showed up and its Ju 87 dive bombers pounded the Soviets with great precision. In order to maximize the effect of their raids, the Axis assault planes operated in large groups (30-60-80 machines). They were escorted by 6-18 Bf 109 fighters. In some occasions larger fighter groups (up to 30 machines) were employed.[55]

# THE GERMAN COUNTEROFFENSIVES

Having neutralized the danger on his right flank, Schörner now turned his attention to the sector of *Armeegruppe Dumitrescu*, which main line of resistance was running mostly along the western bank of the Dniester. There the Soviets had established several bridgeheads that now threatened to become jump-off points for the summer offensive of 3rd Ukrainian Front. That's why they had to be eliminated as quickly as possible.

The series of local offensives were carried out almost exclusively by the German component of *Armeegruppe Dumitrescu* – General de Angelis' 6. Army. Since its divisions were not fully reconstituted after the debacle in the Ukraine, de Angelis employed only their combat-worthy elements, combining them into strong task forces (similar to the Soviet "shock" groups). They were fully supported by the entire might of the available heavy artillery and Luftwaffe.

At first Germans struck the Butor bridgehead (east of Kishinev), which had just been occupied by General Chuikov's 8th Guards Army. [56] In the early hours of 10 May it was attacked by two corps' groups with a total of up to eight divisions (or

their elements) between them. [57] With the crucial help of the close-support aircraft and the friendly artillery, by 12 May the bridgehead was smashed. Chuikov, the celebrated hero of Stalingrad, sustained a terrible defeat. The divisions reported the taking of 3,050 prisoners and a considerable amount of booty (447 artillery pieces, 193 mortars, 380 machineguns, 106 flamethrowers and 102 anti-tank rifles.) [58]

It is worth mentioning the way the attackers utilized their armor. They assembled all available AFVs – twenty or so Pz IV tanks, a handful of halftracks and the assault guns of Brigade 911 into a provisional armored battle group under the leadership of 3. Panzer-Division. By doing so they were able to deliver a powerful blow in a narrow sector and penetrate the Soviet defense at once.

\* \* \*

De Angelis gave the Russians no time for respite. On the very next day after destruction of the Butor bridgehead (13 May) he attacked the one at Răscăieţi (south of Tiraspol) with two infantry divisions. [59] The assault began early in the morning, before dawn, in order to nullify the Soviet artillery superiority. The Germans employed their favorite method of warfare – strong "shock" detachments supported by aircraft and handful of AFVs. Once again the occupants of the foothold (320th Rifle Division of 6th Army) were caught off guard and defeated. By nightfall they retreated to the eastern bank leaving behind more than 1,200 dead bodies, 44 artillery pieces, 44 machineguns and 30 anti-tank rifles; about 750 of them were taken prisoner. [60]

The battle for the Koshnitsa bridgehead, which was situated to the northeast of Kishinev, between Butor and Dubossary, lasted much longer, but eventually the German managed to eliminate it, too. At first, it was the Soviets (5th Shock Army) who prevailed. They attacked during the night of 13/14 May and secured most of the foothold, pushing back a regiment of 4. Mountain Division. But on 15 and 16 May the Germans counterattacked simultaneously the both flanks of the Soviet penetration corridor with the combined forces of two panzer and one infantry divisions [61] and cut off the ground communications of the opponent. An entire Soviet rifle corps was

55   TsAMO, fu. 327, inv. 4999, f. 157, pp. 97-101.

56   The bridgehead was taken over in the first days of May 1944 from 5th Guards Army of 2nd Ukrainian Front.

57   LII. Army Corps (*General der Infanterie* Erich Buschenhagen) and XXXX. Panzer Corps (General der Panzertruppen Otto von Knobelsdorff); 3., 13. and 14. Panzer-Divisions; 294. and 320. Infantry Divisions; 2. Parachute Division; a battle group of 17. Infantry Division and a regiment of 4. Mountain Division.

58   NARA T312/1469/000280.

59   9. and 258. Infantry Divisions of XXIX. Army Corps.

60   NARA T312/1469/000280.

61   13. and 14. Panzer-Divisions (18 tanks altogether); 335. Infantry Division.

*A Panther Ausf. A tank destroyed during the German 1944 summer counteroffensives in Rumania. (RGAKFD)*

trapped inside. [62] Mopping up the pocket lasted till 21 May. Part of the encircled Soviets managed to break out, but at the cost of heavy losses. The victorious troops of the German LII. Army Corps reported yet another major victory. About 1,900 prisoners were taken, alongside with 71 artillery pieces and 231 machineguns. 44 tanks were reportedly destroyed and more than 4,000 dead bodies were counted on the battlefield. [63]

Thus ended the spring "bridgehead" mini-campaign of the resurrected 6. Army. It deserves a much more detailed study not only because it was one of the last German victories of the war, but also because of tactical skills displayed by both frontline troops and their commanders. The latter however, made one major mistake – they didn't eliminate the large Soviet bridgehead at Chițcani (Kitskany) and, as we will see later, this would have fatal consequences for the fate of the entire Army Group "South Ukraine".

**CLAIMS OF 6. ARMY FOR 1-31 MAY 1944
DESTROYED OR/AND CAPTURED:**

- 68 tanks
- 4 SU-76M self-propelled guns
- 3 other types self-propelled guns
- 18 aircraft
- 603 artillery pieces (including AT and AA guns)
- 239 mortars
- 772 machineguns
- 286 flamethrowers.[64]

\* \* \*

The culmination of Schörner's offensive efforts in Rumania were two operations with tender names – "Katja" and "Sonja". They were launched by General Wöhler's 8. Army in the vicinity of Iași with the objective of destroying a probable Soviet buildup north of the city. Intelligence had identified large enemy troop concentrations

*Erich Hartmann, Luftwaffe top-scoring fighter ace. (NAC)*

---

62    34th Guards Rifle Corps with two rifle divisions, a tank brigade and parts of an artillery division.
63    NARA T312/1469/000282.
64    NARA T312/1469/000282.

*Heinz Frank and Gerhard Barkhorn (right) were two of the most prominent fighter pilots of Air Fleet 4 in the spring of 1944. (NAC)*

there and Schörner decided to form a Panzer task force to attack and destroy them. These limited-scale operations turned out to be one of few major offensives to be conducted by the Wehrmacht during 1944 on the Eastern Front. Moreover, they ignited the last big air battle fought in the East.

The Germans and Rumanians had up to 850 aircraft at their disposal. The Soviet 5th Air Army clearly outnumbered them – it had close to 1,400. Nevertheless, the battle rather ended in a draw. What is more impressive than the numbers is perhaps the fact that for the first and last time during the war, all prominent Eastern Front aces - Hartmann, Barkhorn, Lipfert, Rudel, Kozhedub, Pokryshkin, Rechkalov – met in the air.

The battle opened on 30 May. At first, the Axis pilots prevailed. The close-support aircraft of Air Fleet 4 hit hard the Soviet ground positions. But right from the outset they encountered fierce opposition. The tank-busting ace Rudel recalls it:

> Our missions now take us into a relatively stabilized sector where, however, the gradual arrival of reinforcements indicates that the Reds are preparing a thrust into the heart of Rumania. Our operational area extends from the village of Targul Frumos in the west to some bridgeheads over the Dniester S. of Tiraspol in the southeast. Most of our sorties take us into the area north of Jassy between

these points; here the Soviets are trying to oust us from the high ground round Carbiti near the Pruth. The bitterest fighting in this sector rages round the ruins of the castle of Stanca on the so-called Castle Hill. Time and again we lose this position and always recapture it.

In this zone the Soviets are constantly bringing up their stupendous reserves. How often do we attack the river bridges in this area; our route is over the Pruth to the Dniester beyond Kishinew and further east. Koschnitza, Grigoriopol and the bridgehead at Butor are names we shall long remember. For a short period comrades of the 52nd Fighter Wing are stationed with us on our airfield. Their C.O. is Squadron Leader Barkhorn who knows his job from A to Z. They often escort us on our sorties and we give them plenty of trouble, for the new Yak 3, which has made its appearance on the other side, puts up a show every now and then. A group advanced base is operating from Jassy, from where it is easier to patrol the air space above the front. The Group Captain is often up in the front line to observe the cooperation of his formations with the ground troops. His advance post has a wireless set which enables him to pick up all R/T interchanges in the air and on the ground. The fighter pilots talk to one another, the fighters with their control officer, the Stukas among themselves, with their liaison officer on the ground and others. Normally, however, we all use different wave lengths. A little anecdote, which the Group Captain told us on his last visit to our dispersal, shows the extent of his concern for his individual lambs. He was watching our squadron approaching Jassy. We were heading north, our objective being to attack targets in the castle area, which the army wanted neutralized after making contact with our control. We were met over Jassy, not by our own fighters, but by a strong formation of Lags. In a second the sky was full of crazily swerving aircraft. The slow Stukas were ill matched against the arrow-swift Russian fighters, especially as our bomb load further slowed us down. With mixed feelings the Group Captain watched the battle and overheard this conversation. The skipper of the 7th Flight, assuming that I had not seen a Lag 5 which was coming up from below me, called a warning: "Look out, Hannelore, one of them is going to shoot you down!" I had spotted the blighter a long time ago, but there was still ample time to take evasive action. I dislike this yelling over the R/T; it upsets the crews and has a bad effect on accuracy. So I replied: "The one who shoots me down has not yet been born."[65]

65   A. Drabkin (Ed.), "Ya dralsya s Panzerwaffe", Moscow, Yauza-Eksmo, 2007, p. 337.

*This Rumanian Bf 109G-2, fitted with a 300-litre auxiliary belly tank, was photographed in 1944. (Dénes Bernád)*

*Technicians work on the Daimler-Benz DB 605A engine of a Bf 109G on a Rumanian air base, in 1944. (Dénes Bernád)*

*The Rumanian pilot who steps out of the cockpit is Adjutant aviator Ion Enache of Grupul 8 asalt. (Dénes Bernád)*

One of those who were under orders to provide fighter escort for the Stukas was the German fighter pilot Helmut Lipfert, one of the Luftwaffe top-scoring aces. He quickly found out that the quality of his Soviet opponents had improved considerably:

The two *Staffeln* of our *Gruppe* transferred to Husi on the Prut River on May 27. From there we resumed combat flying. Also based at Husi was *Major* Rudel and his Stukas We fighter pilots were given the job of providing escort for the bombers when they flew up to Jassy. In the period, which began on May 31, 1944, I shot down a total of nine enemy aircraft while on escort duties.
We soon learned that there were Russians in this combat zone that could fly as well as we.
My wingman and I approached the front slowly at 2,500 meters, looking to all sides because, because a number of Il-2s had been reported. Then we sighted them, about 1,000 meters below us. As a precaution I looked around one more time before attacking and spotted two enemy machines with red noses coming at us from out of the sun. I quickly instructed my wingman to stay close, but waited and acted as if I hadn't noticed the attackers. When the Russians were in firing range we hauled our machines around into a tight turn. The two Airacobras shot past as they were unable to turn with us due to their greater speed. They didn't give up, however. The two fighters pulled up and came down at us again. They made up one attack after another and forced us ever lower.
The two enemy aircraft became four. Now we had to face constantly alternating attacks and never got an opportunity to fire. My wingman was even hit several times. Then I rammed the throttle forward, pulled the stick back into my stomach and spun down from 1,000 meters almost to ground level. I pulled out and raced away just above the ground toward the southwest. I saw an aircraft at my seven o'clock position and with relief recognized my wingman's "109". He had stayed rightly behind me and had even emulated my spin.
I wasn't about to let the Russians catch us so easily second time, so we climbed quickly t 4,500 meters. But even at that altitude several Airacobras jumped us from above and gave us such a scare that it was not until the flight home that I really recovered my senses. On the third sortie we climbed to 6,000 meters. I had never encountered Russian aircraft a higher altitude. But once again we even didn't reach the front. All I saw was Airacobras above. Once again they forced us to flee. Now I had really had enough, and following a steep Split-S I made my

home with my wingman as fast as I could. I was furious when I landed. Never before had the Russians simply not allowed me to get into attack position. [66]

The improved overall quality of the Soviet pilots was due, to a considerable degree, to the extensive training they had received before the battle - throughout the entire month of May they performed about 7,400 training sorties. Furthermore, 5th Air Army was considerably reinforced – it got the elite 9th Guards Fighter Air Division, which had been equipped with Lend-lease P-39 "Airacobra" fighter planes. Manpower reinforcements also arrived – up to 140 new pilots were introduced to the units. But this was not all. During the quiet period between the Soviet early-May disastrous offensive and the Axis "Katja" counteroffensive dozens of new airfields were built on orders of 5th Air Army's commander, General Goryunov. This made his units far more flexible and maneuverable. Additionally, the army was issued with a large quantity of state-of-the-art equipment, namely ground radars and powerful radios. The cooperation between the units improved and this also had an immediate effect on the work of the forward air controllers.

The improved overall quality of 5th Air Army became apparent already on the first day of the battle, when the Soviet fighter units achieved some pretty impressive results. Thus, a group of Airacobras of 9th Guards Fighter Air Division engaged a large formation of Stukas escorted by Fw 190s and Bf 109s, which was heading towards the Soviet ground positions. In the ensuing dogfight, the Red pilots claimed to have shot down five Ju 87s, three Fw 190s and one Bf 109 without losses of their own. Pokryshkin himself was credited with three Stukas.

But not all aerial engagements were that successful for the Red "falcons". Evgeniy Mariinskiy, a Soviet fighter ace from Pokryshkin's division, tells us about one of them:

Gulayev's second sortie was not that successful. Their 'sixer' [six-plane group] came across eight Messerschmitts, but thirty more Ju-88, escorted by sixteen Me109s, closed in. Our claims made up nine enemy planes, i.e. five 'clodhoppers' and four Messerschmitts, and five more in the whole sortie. But the Germans managed to shoot down the whole 'sixer'. My comrade Akinshin, from aeroclub and flying school, and a young pilot Gromov, who had just joined the Regiment, died. Zadiraka, Chesnokov and Kozinov managed to bail out from burning planes. The same day, being wounded, they returned to the Regiment, from

66    H. Lipfert and W. Girbig, "The War Diary of Hauptmann Helmut Lipfert", Atglen, Schiffer Publishing, 1993, pp. 114-115.

*Some of the top scoring aces of 9th Guards Fighter Air Division (from left to right: Klubov, Rechkalov, Trud, Glinka), Bessarabia, June 1944. (Author's collection)*

From 30 May to 8 June the units of 5th Air Army conducted 5,751 combat sorties. Their losses amounted to 135 machines. The German I. Air Corps, in turn, performed 10,498 sorties, losing 78 aircraft as total write-offs due to various reasons.[69] (No factual information is available on the Rumanian air units.) It was clear that once again the Luftwaffe was the more active part. But the results of the battle cannot be measured in numbers alone. Pretty often the Soviet pilots fought as equals and in several occasions were able to regain the initiative. It was apparent that they were excellent learners and their quality was constantly improving.

\* \* \*

The offensive on the ground was no less bloody than that in the air. Wöhler attacked early in the morning of 30 May with three panzer and one German infantry divisions[70], supported by assault guns, heavy artillery and the already mentioned close air support provided by Luftwaffe. Some Rumanian infantry divisions also took part in the battle.

Right from the outset the Axis assault teams encountered fierce resistance put up by the Soviet 52nd Army. Armin Böttger, a panzer radio operator with 24. Panzer-Division, provides a vivid recollection of those hellish days:

> Now began again those terrible days for German and Russian alike when the Grim Reaper rode along with us. After such a long time together we panzer men naturally knew each other very well: one was more friendly with one, less with another. On the evening of my first attack in this war zone I heard of the death of a radio operator colleague with whom I had spent a lot of time. A shell penetrated the interior of the panzer, killing both the driver and radio operator. Thus fell Unteroffizier Lorenz. After that came blow after blow, just like the story of the Ten Little Nigger Boys, set in brutal reality. Next evening six or seven panzer men sat around a table. Twenty-four hours later five of them were dead, four from one crew alone. One morning seventeen panzers were operational and by the evening only six of twenty-two. From this one could estimate "when one's time would come". […]

where they were sent to a hospital. Gulayev himself was wounded too, but managed to land his plane on a ground attackers' aerodrome. His main mistake was that he had taken three non-battle-seasoned flyers that were shot down in their first combat.[67]

9th Guards Fighter Air Division sustained even more painful losses on the next day, when a formation of Airacobras, this time led by another ace, Grigoriy Rechkalov, were intercepted over Iași by Bf 109s. In the engagement that followed, five of the P-39s were lost.

The nightmarish fighting in the air continued with undiminished ferocity throughout the entire first week of June. It was perhaps best summarized by Mariinskiy:

> Later on everything got mixed up. There were sorties, dogfights, watches on the aerodrome at full alert, short sleeps. To be exact, night-time naps, as we slept no longer than two hours, and sorties, watches and dogfights again. Never before had the Regiment fought battles of such ferocity, or encountered such massive actions by the German aviation.[68]

67    E. Mariinskiy, "Red Star Airacobra", Solihull, Helion & Company, 2006.
68    Ibid.
69    D. Hazanov, "Bitva nad Yassami", Avia Master magazine, 4/1999, p. 26.
70    14., 23. and 24. Panzer-Divisions; 79. Infantry Division.

One of the following evenings our squadron commander notified us of a major offensive for the next day (Operation Sonya, 30 May 1944); "First the artillery will fire, then the Luftwaffe will come with Me 109s and Stukas (Rudel's squadron), preparing the terrain for our panzer attack and to support us. Then the 12th [Squadron] will go forward, and nothing will stop us until we reach the Pruth." We had settled down on our blankets for the night alongside our panzers when suddenly an inferno of fire awoke us from deep sleep. Unknown to us, a multiple rocket projector had been positioned close alongside our panzer. With a great flash of fire and a dreadful long-drawn out detonation it discharged its rockets through the early hours. Was this a good or bad sign? At four in the morning – as promised – the artillery bombardment began, and the German warplanes came to our support. We were positioned on a reverse slope with the grenadiers, who waited in their trenches. Once they had gone forward to the advanced trenches the attack began with the order "Panzers, marsch!"

We had gone only a little way when wire wrapped around the tracks of our panzer and snarled up so badly that we could not run a straight course. We had to get out to free the tracks of the wire and lost valuable time waiting for the wire cutters. Because the terrain was still mined there could be no talk of an easy advance. Opposite us was a slight rise. The Russians could fire at us from an elevated position, and they fired at us "from every buttonhole". We shot back, of course, but never saw a Russian, and had to aim at their muzzle flashes. Our advance stalled, and we remained stuck in an unfavorable position. Then the Russian shells began to fall all around us. My panzer got two shell-hits on a running wheel below the undercarriage. Luckily the Russian aim was not good. Eighty meters away to our flank a panzer of our squadron had been hit and immobilized. A crewman lay on it, half naked, his uniform completely tattered, thigh bleeding, hit by an explosive shell. He was obviously in terrible pain. The back of his leg had spread open like a cauliflower by the explosive effect of this murderous shell. Without asking my commander's permission, I jumped down from our panzer to fetch this wounded comrade. Together with a crewman from the disabled panzer I carried the wounded man over to our panzer and laid him on a blanket on the plating. Despite the padding he felt the heat of the plating and cried out. But where else could we put him? In soaring temperatures our panzer headed at full speed for the back slopes. Alerted by radio, our surgeon came forward immediately in his specially equipped panzer and after examining the casualty gave him no chance of survival. At the same moment another panzer

*Hauptmann Helmuth Ott, a Knight's Cross holder, speaks with a soldier in the trenches near Iaşi, June 1944. His unit (Grenadier-Regiment 97 of 46. Infantry Division) played a key role in halting the Soviet 1944 spring offensive in Rumania. Note the two tank destruction badges worn on the upper right arm of Ott's tunic. (NAC)*

arrived back also carrying a severely wounded man, picked off by an enemy whom we never saw once in this skirmish. There was a large hole in his back, a shell had torn away a large chunk of flesh of two hands' width. The endless agony of death on the battlefield was etched in his green-yellow pallid face. He had been a very rowdy young man, perhaps even a hooligan, but now he only whimpered, "Mother, help, mother help me." The surgeon looked him over and announced that he too would be dead in a short while. [71]

The powerful enemy attack forced Army-General Malinovsky, who had just taken over the command of 2nd Ukrainian Front from Konev, to commit to battle 6th Tank Army (153 tanks and self-propelled guns). Its actions, however, were only partially successful, because nearly all attempts of the army to launch counterattacks were forestalled and intercepted by the Germans. Not surprisingly, its losses mounted and on 31 May alone 43 Soviet tanks became charred and twisted wrecks. [72]

By the end of Day 3 the attackers had succeeded in capturing most of the Soviet positions on the southern bank of the Jijia River. Now Schörner and Wöhler decided to shift the direction of their main attack to the northwest and capture the tactically important heights in that area. Thus, "Katja" became "Sonja".

The formidable Panzer-Grenadier Division "Grossdeutschland" was thrown into the battle already on the first day of the new operation (2 June). Now Malinovsky had no other choice left, but to commit his other tank army – the 2nd – with its 75 tanks and self-propelled guns. Even though the Germans had managed to expel the Russians from most the tactically important hills in the area, their offensive gradually began to lose momentum. In the evening of 6 June the exhausted and worn-out panzer and infantry formations went over to the defensive.[73]

General der Infanterie Kurt Röpke (the commander of 46. Infantry Division) and General Nicolae Stoenescu (the commander of the Rumanian IV. Army Corps) observe the Soviet positions at Iași, May 1944. The picture clearly shows the tactical importance of the commanding hills northwest of Iași. (NAC)

## THE CRIMEA

The situation on the extreme right flank of Army Group "South Ukraine" was completely different. The 17. Army of *Generaloberst* Erwin Jaenecke, which had been trapped in Crimea in the first days of November 1943, had little chance of

survival against the massed onslaught of 4th Ukrainian Front that began on 8 April 1944. The forces led by Army-General Tolbukhin relentlessly pushed forward and in a matter of one week reached Sevastopol, Jaenecke's main base and supply point. The badly mauled German and Rumanian divisions were ordered to make a stand there, but it was clear to everyone that it was not going to last long. The desperate commander of 17. Army flew to Hitler's HQ in Berchtesgaden to convince the Fuehrer that immediate and total evacuation was necessary, but the dictator remained unmoved. Worse still, Hitler burst into a rage, relieved the unfortunate Jaenecke and replaced him with *General der Infanterie* Karl Allmendinger. But this didn't save the army from the looming disaster. Shortly afterwards Tolbukhin struck again and on

71   Böttger, op. cit.
72   TsAMO, fu. 240, inv. 2779, f. 1161, p. 9.
73   TsAMO, fu. 240, inv. 2779, f. 1161, p. 11.

9 May Sevastopol was liberated. By 12 May the last Axis pockets of resistance were eliminated and the Soviets restored their control over the entire peninsula. Even though Kriegsmarine, Luftwaffe the Rumanian Royal Navy managed to evacuate more than 120,000 men (out of 230,000), 17. Army no longer possessed even a bit of its previous fighting capacity.

The change of the rule in Crimea did have long term consequences for many. For instance, it shook the political position of the Third Reich in the entire region. Already on 20 April, when Sevastopol was still in German hands, Turkey agreed to cease the export of chromium, a valuable strategic raw material, to the Third Reich's arms industry. But the Soviet victory affected not only certain economic and diplomatic relations, it also had a direct impact on the lives of entire ethnic groups. Thus, from 18 to 20 May 1944 no less than 250,000 Crimean Tartars (mostly women, children, the elderly) were forcibly deported to Uzbekistan using cattle trains. About a month later they were followed by other local minorities – Bulgarians, Greeks and Armenians. Thus they shared the fate of hundreds of thousands of Caucasians (Kalmyks, Karachays, Chechens, Ingush, Balkars) who had been expulsed to Central Asia several months earlier. These deportations ostensibly were intended as collective punishment for the perceived collaboration of the ethnic groups in question with the Nazi occupiers. However, it is quite possible that they were part of Stalin's plan to cleanse the border regions of hypothetical rebellious nations. After all, the Soviet Union was preparing for a war with Turkey for the straits of the Bosporus and the Dardanelles and the "cleansing" of the Caucasus and Crimea in 1943-1944 was presumably one of the preliminary moves.

# THE QUIET TIMES

Throughout most of the summer of 1944 Army Group "South Ukraine" enjoyed a quiet period of rest and recuperation. On 22 June 1944, when Stalin unleashed his biggest summer offensive – Operation "Bagration" in Byelorrusia – General Walter Wenck – Schörner's chief of staff – reported that Army Group "South Ukraine" was in excellent condition.

By the beginning of July the entire Eastern Front, save for the Rumanian sector was ablaze, and Hitler began to pull out division after division from Schörner. Worse still, most of the Luftwaffe units, which had proven themselves instrumental in

checking the Soviet armored avalanches, flew to the north, too. Schörner, however, had no time to worry about the weakening of his armies, because immediately after the failed assassination attempt against him, Hitler ordered him to swap to commands with *Generaloberst* Johannes Friessner, the commander of the hardly pressed Army Group "North".

Within hours after the bomb exploded on 20 July the Fuehrer sacked the Chief of the General Staff Kurt Zeitzler. His successor, *Generaloberst* Heinz Guderian, found himself in a midst of a great chaos. He had to quickly reassemble a functioning General Staff and at the same time to rebuild the crumbling fronts of the badly mauled Army Groups "Center" and "North Ukraine". Within two weeks five panzer and six infantry divisions were boarded on trains and urgently transferred to the most critical points of the Eastern Front. Thus, by the beginning of August 1944 Army Group "South Ukraine" was left with only two weak armored divisions that were to fulfill the role of mobile operational reserves: 13. Panzer-Division and 10. Panzer-Grenadier-Division. Neither of them had more than 40 tanks or assault guns.

After the war Guderian explained his decisions this way:

Our strongest force seemed to be Army Group South Ukraine, which consisted of the Sixth and Eighth Armies as well as Rumanian troops and a portion of the Hungarian Army. Its front ran from the mouth of the Dnieper on the Black Sea coast—along that river to a point south of Kichinev—north of Jassy—south of Falticeni—across the rivers Pruth and Sereth—and finally north-west to the Sereth's catchment area. During the spring battles in March and April, this army group had succeeded in defeating enemy attacks north of Jassy and had finally managed to withdraw a number of divisions into reserve. It was at this time commanded by General Schörner, who enjoyed Hitler's special confidence. […] My predecessor left me not only a disorganized staff, but also a completely disintegrating front. There were no reserves available to the OKH. The only forces immediately to hand were those in Rumania behind Army Group South Ukraine. A glance at a railway map will show that it was bound to take a considerable time to move them up. The limited forces that could be produced by the Training Army were already on their way to the generally beaten Army Group Center. In agreement with the commander of Army Group South Ukraine, whose chief of staff, General Wenck, now became my principal operational assistant and who knew the situation in Rumania well, I proposed to Hitler that all divisions

*Generaloberst Johannes Friessner, the Commander-in-Chief of Army Group "South Ukraine". (NARA)*

that could be made available in Rumania be moved away from there and be used to plug the gap between Army Groups Center and North. This was agreed at once. Hitler also ordered that the commanders of Army Groups South Ukraine (Schörner) and North (Friessner) exchange posts. Instructions were issued to the new commander of Army Group South Ukraine which, for Hitler, allowed that officer unusual latitude of decision.[74]

Friessner not only inherited a crippled army group. He himself could not match Schörner as master of defensive warfare. Worse still, Friessner and his staff failed to spot the Soviet troop buildup along the main line of resistance. The leadership of Army Group "South Ukraine", as well as the German military mission in Bucharest, made another critical omission: they ignored the signs that their Rumanian ally was preparing to change sides.

Guderian later wrote about that in his memoir:

On 5 August, 1944, while we were preoccupied by the events connected with the assassination attempt and by the collapse of the Eastern Front, Marshal Antonescu, the Head of the Rumanian State, had appeared at Hitler's headquarters in East Prussia. I was instructed to brief the Marshal on the state of the Eastern Front. Hitler, Keitel, and the others who usually attended such briefings were present, as well as Ribbentrop and his assistants from the Ministry for Foreign Affairs. During the conference Antonescu showed that he fully grasped the difficulties of our situation and the need for reforming, first of all, Army Group Center's front and then for re-establishing contact between Army Groups Center and North. He proposed himself that Moldavia be evacuated and that we withdraw to a line Galatz-Focsani-the Carpathian Mountains, if the common interests of the allied powers should make such a withdrawal desirable. I immediately translated this

magnanimous offer to Hitler and reminded him of it again later. Hitler gratefully accepted Antonescu's offer and - as will be seen - drew certain conclusions from it. The next morning Antonescu invited me to his quarters in the Wolfsschanze for a private conversation alone with him. I found this talk most instructive. The Rumanian Marshal showed that he was not only a good soldier, but also displayed an exact knowledge of his country, its communications and economic conditions, as well as of the political necessities. Everything he said was based on solid common sense and was expressed with amiability and courtesy, qualities to which at that time we in Germany were not exactly accustomed. He soon began to speak of the attempted assassination and did not try to disguise how deeply it had shocked him. 'Believe me, I can have implicit faith in every one of my generals. The idea of officers taking part in such a coup d'état is unthinkable to us!' At the time I could not reply to these serious reproaches. But fourteen days later Antonescu was to be faced with a very different situation, and we with him. Among those who had accompanied the Marshal on this visit was the Rumanian Foreign Minister, Michai Antonescu. This man gave the impression of slyness and was not an attractive charmer. His friendliness seemed to have a rather slimy quality. With them they had brought the German Ambassador to Rumania, Killinger, and the head of the German military mission in that country, General Hansen. I had lengthy conversations with both these men concerning their opinions. Neither of them thought a great deal of Antonescu, but believed that the Germans should support the young king as the figurehead of the Rumanian state. In this they were making a serious mistake, which was to involve the German military authorities in a quite false sense of security, as a result of which the scattered reports we received of intended treachery were not evaluated correctly. At the end of July Colonel-General Freissner had succeeded Schörner as commander of Army Group South Ukraine; he now agreed with Antonescu's suggestions and shortly after the latter's visit to Supreme Headquarters he proposed to Hitler that our front be withdrawn to the line Galatz-Focsani-the Carpathian Mountains. Hitler, with certain reservations, agreed, but insisted that he must receive clear proof of the enemy's intentions to attack before he would issue the necessary orders for the withdrawal and before any such movement be begun. Until that time the present front must continue to be held. Intelligence received at Supreme Headquarters concerning the situation in Rumania during the next few days was highly confused and contradictory: in general—owing to the attitude of the responsible German authorities in that

74    H. Guderian, "Panzer Leader", London, Macdonald Futura Publishers, 1980, pp. 352-354.

country - it was favorable. All the same the Foreign Minister, von Ribbentrop, had such a deep lack of confidence in the reports sent him by his ambassador that he believed it necessary to transfer a panzer division to Bucharest and requested Hitler that this be done. I was present when this matter was discussed and I decided Ribbentrop's attitude was the correct one. But I could not make a division available from among those that were engaged on the Eastern Front, for the situation there was far too critical already. I therefore proposed that the 4th SS Polizei Division be withdrawn from fighting the guerrillas in Serbia and used for this more urgent task in Rumania. This was a motorized division and could therefore reach the Rumanian capital with the requisite speed. But Jodl declared that the division was not available, even though Wallachia at that time was one of the so-called OKW theatres of war and, as it did not count as part of the Eastern Front, was therefore directly under Jodl's authority. Hitler could not make up his mind. Nothing was done.[75]

\* \* \*

Stalin ordered 2nd and 3rd Ukrainian Front to begin the planning of their summer offensives on 2 August. By then both fronts already had been massively reinforced with men and materiel. More importantly, the Soviet commanders had a plenty of time to train their troops, as well as to analyze previous mistakes. Even though three all-arms armies and two tanks armies had left for the Ukraine and Poland, the remaining formations had been brought up to full strength and now were super-strong. Both Fronts, for instance, had nearly 1,900 tanks and self-propelled guns at their disposal, while Friessner could field against them only 400 or so. The situation in the air was even more disadvantageous for the Axis side: 5th and 17th Air Armies had about 1,800 combat aircraft altogether, save for the Soviet Black Sea Fleet, which also had about 500. The German Air Fleet 4 could oppose them with only 232 serviceable combat planes, the Royal Rumanian Air Force had even less.

The plan of the Soviet Supreme Command called for coordinated simultaneous attacks by 2nd and 3rd Ukrainian Fronts, in close cooperation with the Black Sea Fleet. To destroy the main body of Axis troops in the Iaşi - Kishinev – Bendery area, and subsequently to advance deep in to Rumania to take Bucharest and the Ploesti oil region. The breakthrough attacks were to be accompanied by secondary attacks in the adjacent sectors, thereby preventing the Axis commanders from shifting troops to the points of the main Soviet efforts.

The 2nd Ukrainian Front was to deliver its main blow with 27th Army in the area north of Iaşi. Then it was to commit 18th Tank Corps, 6th Tank Army and Major-General Gorshkov's Cavalry Mechanized Group. The assignment of the former was to seize the Prut River crossings in the deep rear of *Armeegruppe Dumitrescu*; the latter two were to race southwestwards and capture the Siret River crossings, and the vital pass known as the "Focşani Gap", where the Rumanians had built a solid fortified line and where the Axis command intended to make a stand. By doing so, a further dash by 6th Tank Army to Bucharest would be facilitated.

The 3rd Ukrainian Front was to launch its main concentrated attack with 37th Army from the Chiţcani (Kitskany) bridgehead, the only Soviet foothold that was not destroyed during the German "anti-bridgehead" campaign in May 1944. Upon breaching the Axis defense in the Bendery – Tiraspol area, the army commander was to release his main exploitation forces – 4th Guards and 7th Mechanized Corps – for a deep raid. Upon breaking into open country, both corps would turn north and

*A Hummel heavy self-propelled howitzer of 13. Panzer-Division destroyed by the Shturmoviks of 17th Air Army in the vicinity of Tokuz, Bessarabia, 21 August 1944. (TsAMO)*

75   Guderian, op. cit., pp. 364-366.

link up with 18<sup>th</sup> Tank Corps of 2<sup>nd</sup> Ukrainian Front, thereby encircling the main body of Axis forces in the Kishinev area. The new Front commander, Army-General Tolbukhin, was now given the opportunity to prove his reputation of being a master of mobile warfare.

# THE JASSY-KISHINEV OPERATION

The final Soviet offensive in Rumania began early in the morning of 20 August. In the sector of 3<sup>rd</sup> Ukrainian Front the assault didn't proceed as planned, because the Germany infantry divisions offered a very determined resistance. On the top of that, the Kitskany bridgehead was way too small to contain a heavily reinforced "shock" group. 7<sup>th</sup> Mechanized Corps, for instance, became stuck among the friendly infantry and supply columns, and its introduction to battle was delayed for several critical hours on 20/21 August. Further problems occurred when on 21 August the sole mobile reserve of *Armeegruppe Dumitrescu*; launched a fierce counterattack. Tolbukhin, however, reacted very quickly and employed the entire firepower available in this sector, as well as the full might of the Il-2 'Shturmoviks' of 17<sup>th</sup> Air Army against the panzers. By the end of the day the unfortunate panzer-division was literally shot to pieces. It was only on 22 August when Tolbukhin's armies achieved a clean breakthrough in the Bendery – Tiraspol area.

In the Iași sector the Axis main line of resistance was nearly vaporized by the artillery barrages of 2<sup>nd</sup> Ukrainian Front already in the morning hours of 20 August.

Vasili Bryukhov, a company commander with 18<sup>th</sup> Tank Corps, recalls the entry of his unit into the battle:

> Our artillery had pounded the German defenses to such an extent that we could barely drive over the ground – the former front line was like a moonscape, there were so many shell craters. So for the first fifteen kilometers there was no opposition from the Germans at all. We only encountered organized resistance at their second line of defense along the Valuislui River. But by the end of the first day we were already behind the German lines. There was no longer a recognizable front line, just pockets of resistance. [76]

*A Hummel heavy self-propelled howitzer of 13. Panzer-Division destroyed by the Shturmoviks of 17<sup>th</sup> Air Army, Bessarabia in the vicinity of Tokuz, 21 August 1944. (TsAMO)*

To increase the weight of his onslaught Malinovsky released 6<sup>th</sup> Tank Army already on the first day of the offensive. The Axis defense quickly collapsed, especially because some of the Rumanian units put up halfhearted resistance at best. Of course, there were exceptions. 10. Panzer-Grenadier-Division, for instance, fought back with great vigor. Its brilliant rearguard action in the vicinity of Iași allowed many Axis units to

*A Pz IV Ausf. J tank of 6./Panzer-Regiment 4 (13. Panzer-Division) destroyed by the Shturmoviks of 17<sup>th</sup> Air Army, Bessarabia, 22 August 1944. (TsAMO)*

38

76   A. Drabkin and O. Sheremet (Eds.), "T-34 in Action", Mechanicsburg, Stackpole Books, 2008 pp. 139-140.

avoid entrapment. But everything was in vain. On 23 August those factions in the Rumanian leadership that opposed Antonescu carried out a coup and the Marshal was arrested in the Royal Palace in Bucharest. Rumania officially changed sides and the German divisions of Army Group "South Ukraine" were left alone on the battlefield.

The rapid Soviet advance and the Rumanian turnabout led to the forming of two large pockets, in which five corps of both German armies were trapped. The first one, which emerged in the vicinity of Kishinev, contained three corps of 6. Army; the other one, which was smaller, held captive two corps of 8. Army between the rivers Prut and Siret. Despite the critical situation, their divisions and battle groups were still able to maintain some semblance of order. They moved in long columns to the west and southwest, still hoping for a miraculous breakout. But the Soviets gave them no chance.

The Luftwaffe was nowhere to be seen. Air Fleet 4 had attempted to strike back during the first two days of the battle, but the Soviet superiority in numbers began to tell and after 22 August both air armies were in complete control of the cloudless August sky. From then on Shturmoviks, Bostons, Lavochkins and Yaks, bombed and strafed the Axis ground troops without mercy. It is no wonder that after 23

*An Sd.Kfz. 8 prime mover destroyed by 17th Air Army in Bessarabia, 21 August 1944. (TsAMO)*

*An Sd.Kfz. 11 prime mover of one of the German infantry divisions fully destroyed by a group of 4 Shturmoviks of 17th Air Army in the vicinity of the village of Borodino, Bessarabia, 22 August 1944. (TsAMO)*

*An RSO tractor destroyed by 17th Air Army in Bessarabia, 22 August 1944. (TsAMO)*

August it was the retreating German columns that became the favorite targets of the Soviet airmen.

The remnants of the two German armies kept trying to escape and stubbornly attacked to the west and southwest. It was not until 5 September that the last floating pockets of resistance were finally crushed. It was a terrible defeat for the Third Reich.

*Soviet infantrymen of 2nd Ukrainian Front dismount from a T-34 tank during the opening phase of Jassy–Kishinev Operation, late August 1944. (Author's collection)*

*A Soviet OT-34 flamethrower tank of 3rd Ukrainian Front accompanied by infantry during the opening phase of Jassy–Kishinev Operation, late August 1944. (Author's collection)*

Sixteen very experienced infantry divisions perished, the Wehrmacht lost no less than 286,000 men in killed or captured.

Guderian's postwar recollection perhaps summarizes best the view of the German High Command on the catastrophe in Rumania:

On 20 August 1944, the Russians launched their attack against Army Group South Ukraine. This was successful against those sectors that were held by Rumanian troops. But that was not all; the Rumanians deserted in large numbers to the enemy and turned their guns against their allies of yesterday. Neither the German troops nor their leaders had reckoned on such treachery. Although Hitler immediately authorized the withdrawal of the Army Group's front, the troops attempted to hold out in places and to carry out a fighting retreat step by step. In order to avoid a complete collapse and consequent annihilation an immediate withdrawal and rapid seizure of the bridges over the Danube were essential. As this was not done, the Rumanians reached that river before the Germans, closed the crossing-places, and thus left their former allies at the mercy of the Russians. Sixteen German divisions were completely destroyed, an irreplaceable loss in view of our already very difficult situation. These German soldiers fought valiantly to the bitter end; their military honor was unsullied. They were in no way responsible for their sad fate. The misfortune could only have been avoided if the decision to withdraw to the line Galatz-Focsani-the Carpathian Mountains had been implemented before ever the Russians launched their attack; the whole Russian plan would thus have been forestalled and we should have been in possession of a line so shortened that we could have held it even without the assistance of the Rumanians. But to take such a decision required a clear grasp of the political situation and of the morals of the Rumanian leaders. Antonescu himself had been grossly deceived concerning the nature of his organization, and he paid for his mistake with his life. The reliance he placed on his generals and officers was unfortunately unjustified; but it had made a certain impression on the German leaders, with the result that they too were deceived. Within a few weeks Rumania was lost.[77]

77  Guderian, op. cit., p. 367.

*M4A2 Sherman tanks of 5th Mechanized Corps (6th Tank Army) drive through a Rumanian village during the Jassy-Kishinev offensive, late-August 1944. (Bulgarian Military Photo Archive)*

*M4A2 Sherman tank of 5th Mechanized Corps (6th Tank Army) in Bucharest, 31 August 1944. (RiP)*

*M4A2 Sherman tank of 5th Mechanized Corps (6th Tank Army) in Bucharest, 31 August 1944. (RiP)*

*T-34/85 tank of 5th Guards Tank Corps (6th Tank Army) in Bucharest, 31 August 1944. (RiP)*

*T-34/85 tank of 5th Guards Tank Corps (6th Tank Army) in Bucharest, 31 August 1944. (RiP)*

*T-34/85 tanks of 5ᵗʰ Guards Tank Corps (6ᵗʰ Tank Army) in Bucharest, 31 August 1944. (RiP)*

*T-34/85 tank of 5th Guards Tank Corps (6th Tank Army) in Bucharest, 31 August 1944. (RiP)*

*T-34/85 tanks in downtown Bucharest, 31 August 1944. (Author's collection)*

*Mk IX Valentine tanks of 6th Tank Army in Bucharest, 31 August 1944. (Author's collection)*

# CHAPTER 2

# BULGARIA

## THE END OF THE "PASSIVE ALLIANCE"

During World War II Bulgaria remained the only Axis state that didn't join Hitler's anti-Bolshevik crusade and even maintained diplomatic relations with the USSR throughout most of the conflict. On the other hand, in December 1941 it was forced by the Third Reich to declare war on the United Kingdom and the United States, which remained a "phony" one for awhile.

The Bulgarian Kingdom served the interests of Nazi Germany mainly by supplying the Wehrmacht with raw materials and agricultural produce, as well as by providing troops for occupational duties in Serbia and Northern Greece. In turn, King Boris III was allowed to recover some traditional historical territories as Macedonia and Western Thrace.

Bulgaria was definitely one of Hitler's strangest allies. There was no strong Nazi-like party in the country, nor any significant Fascist movements. Anti-Semitic feelings were not widespread and this allowed virtually the entire populace to unite in March 1943 and save the Jews of Bulgarian proper from deportation to the extermination camps. (The Jews from the newly acquired territories, however, could not be spared and nearly all of them perished in the camps.) The Communist Party was rather unpopular, let alone that it was banned. There was some partisan activity (sponsored and supported by Moscow), but it was never as widespread as in the Balkan countries occupied by Germany and Italy.

Hitler himself was traditionally suspicious towards his allies. In his private conversations he repeatedly called King Boris a "cunning fox" and in 1942 made the following observation:

History is a most untrustworthy guide. The Bulgarians are now behaving as if the developments in the Balkans were all the results of their own decisive action. In reality, Boris, caught between his cupidity on the one side and his cowardice on the other, was so hesitant that the strongest intervention on our part was necessary to make him do anything at all. Old Ferdinand wrote some very straight letters, too, pointing out that the hour of Bulgaria's destiny had struck. These Balkan people are quite extraordinary, and they have an astonishing gift for languages.[78]

At the same time he openly admired Boris' father, the old King Ferdinand:

When I recall the German potentates, I find each one more futile than the other. I make one solitary exception—the Tsar of Bulgaria. He was a man of infinite wisdom, inexhaustible tact and unique force of character. Had we had a man like Ferdinand on the throne of Germany, the First World War would never have been fought.[79]

The Fuehrer considered the Bulgarians a combat-worthy ally and openly included them in his strategic plans for repelling a potential Anglo-American invasion in the Balkans:

51

---

footnote
78   H. Trevor-Roper, "Hitler's Table Talk, 1941-1944", Enigma Books, New York, 2000, p. 630.
79   Ibid., p. 647.

*Troops of 3ʳᵈ Ukrainian Front enter Sofia, mid-September 1944. (RiP)*

*Troops of 3ʳᵈ Ukrainian Front enter Sofia, mid-September 1944. (RiP)*

*Troops of 3ʳᵈ Ukrainian Front enter Sofia, mid-September 1944. (RiP)*

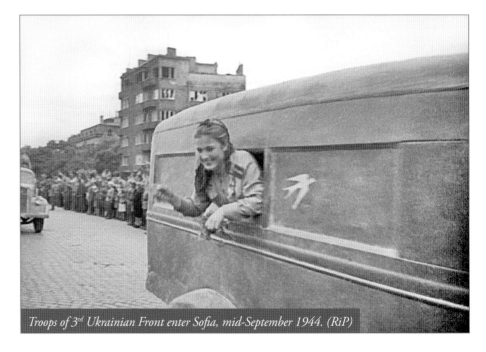

*Troops of 3ʳᵈ Ukrainian Front enter Sofia, mid-September 1944. (RiP)*

*Troops of 3rd Ukrainian Front enter Sofia, mid-September 1944. (RiP)*

*Troops of 3rd Ukrainian Front enter Sofia, mid-September 1944. (RiP)*

It [an Allied invasion] won't be possible in the West, where the defensive positions have been consolidated and improved. If they plan an attack, they will attack only in Italy and the Balkans, of course. The Balkans are dangerous. We have to take everything in consideration. If something happens in Turkey and we have to pull out forces from the East anyway, I will be left with only one reserve to fall back on there – the Bulgarians.[80]

Some of the German senior officers also held a high opinion on Bulgarians in general. In May 1943, for instance, *Feldmarschall* Keitel made the following statement, which was shaped to a considerable degree by the valiant performance of the Bulgarian Army on the battlefields of the First World War:

I have just examined the delivery lists for Bulgaria. No problems, really. We still have to give them tanks. […] everything else, including ammunition and weapons, was shipped to Bulgaria. Yet I would suggest, for the third stage of the main shipment, to continue supplying them, because beside the Finns, the Bulgarians – provided they have arms – are the best fighters we have. They were excellent in the Great War. They are brave, a peasant nation. If they get good weapons, we can count on their assistance.[81]

\* \* \*

On 28 August 1943 King Boris died suddenly at age 49 of apparent heart failure. He was succeeded by his six-year-old son Simeon II, under a three-man Regency Council headed by Boris's brother, Prince Kyril (Cyril). Two of the regents - Kiril and Lieutenant-General Nikola Mikhov of the Royal Bulgarian Army - were mere figureheads and thus the third regent, the pro-German Prime Minister Bogdan Filov became de facto head of state. The latter used his power to appoint Dobri Bozhilov (another Germanophile) prime minister.

In the meantime, the fortunes of the Third Reich and the other Axis nations on the battlefields declined. The balance on the Eastern Front shifted decisively in the favor of the Red Army and in September 1943 the Anglo-American armies landed in mainland Italy. Now the Western Allies had a large airbase, from which to strike at the heart of Nazi Empire.

80   H. Heiber and D. Glantz (Eds.), "Hitler and His Generals", Enigma Books, New York, 2003, p. 131.
81   Ibid., pp. 131-132.

Bulgaria was also not spared. In mid-November 1943 the daylight bombers of Fifteenth Air Force delivered the first (of many) disastrous air raid on Sofia. It was followed by ten more (including some RAF night raids). Bulgarian fighter pilots fought desperately against the invaders, shooting down and damaging dozens of "Liberators", "Flying Fortresses", "Lightnings" and "Mustangs". Their super-human efforts and self-sacrifice, however, were in vain – often outnumbered by ratio of 7 to 1, they were not able to prevent the armadas from dropping their deadly loads on the beautiful city.

The ultimate goal of these Allied raids was to force Bulgaria to leave the Axis camp. And they nearly succeeded. The morale of Bulgarians hit bottom, their capital laid in ruins and it was clear to everyone that Bozhilov's government could not protect the country from Anglo-American punishment.

At the beginning of 1944 the Bulgarian rulers initiated peace talks with the Allies. Contacts were established with the American mission in Turkey. The secret negotiations, however, led to nothing. Many reasons can be cited for their failure, but the main one seems to be the fear of unconditional surrender (demanded by the Allies) and the subsequent German reprisals that were very likely to follow, since there were no British or American troops nearby.

The strategy of the Allies towards Bulgaria was not fair, either, because they had no desire to send troops to the Balkans. Their master plan was to force the Germans to do so. If Bulgaria could be bombed out of the war, Allied chief planners expected that Hitler would then have to occupy the country with troops urgently needed elsewhere. This plan is clearly evident in a report by the British Air Marshal Sir John Slessor:

> The best service we in this theatre can perform for [Operation] Overlord is really to create hell in the Balkans by any means, air, land, and sea that can be made available without embarking on major operations involving bridgeheads that have to be covered and supplied. ...
>
> It appears certain that if the Balkan satellites are knocked out, the effect on German strategy would be catastrophic; and therefore, if heavy bombing seems likely to put them out, which I believe it would, the Hun would have to occupy them or accept their collapse, and he could not afford to do the latter.[82]

82    M. L. Miller, "Bulgaria during the Second World War", Stanford, Stanford University Press, 1975, pp. 169-170.

* * *

If there was one man who was clearly against the peace talks it was Stalin. Like his predecessors, the Russian tsars and emperors, the Soviet dictator considered Bulgaria to be part of his sphere of influence, because of its close proximity to the Turkish Straits.

Already in November 1940, during the Hitler – Molotov meetings in Berlin, it became clear that the Balkans had turned into the apple of discord between the Third Reich and the USSR, with Stalin trying to secure his dominance in Bulgaria to counterpoise the strengthening Nazi positions in Hungary and Rumania, as well as to change in his favor the regime of the Turkish Straits.

But this was not all. Later that month, Stalin offered King Boris to sign a mutual assistance pact permitting Soviet bases to be established in the country in exchange for Soviet support to the Bulgarian territorial claims in Greece and Yugoslavia. Boris and his aides, rightfully suspecting a trap similar that used by Moscow to annex the Baltic countries, rejected the offer.

Following the German invasion of USSR in June 1941, the Moscow-backed Bulgarian Communist Party began to organize resistance groups aiming to form a wide-spread partisan movement. In total disrespect to Bulgaria's non-involvement in Operation "Barbarossa", the Soviet Union immediately gave them full-scale support. Agents were landed from submarines or were dropped by parachute onto Bulgarian territory. (These agents were usually Bulgarian Communists who had been in exile in the Soviet Union and had received an extensive training there.) All landings made on the Bulgarian coast in August and September 1941, however, were unsuccessful, because the agents were apprehended on arrival or were quickly betrayed. The failure of the local peasants and villagers to assist the Communist agents came as a shocking surprise to Moscow, which had also underestimated the alertness of Bulgarian army patrols. Only very few of the landed agents were able to make contact with the resistance movement, but most of them were soon arrested, too.

In the meantime both countries waged an undeclared war in the westernmost part of the Black Sea. From the beginning of August 1941 Soviet submarines began to attack Axis ships in the Bulgarian territorial waters. The Bulgarian High Command responded to this new threat by mobilizing its insufficient air and naval forces. Closely cooperating with the German convoys, the Bulgarian crews and pilots contributed to the sinking of up to 5-6 Soviet submarines.

*Pz IV Ausf. H tanks of the Bulgarian Armored Brigade in front of the National Theatre in Sofia shortly after the coup, mid-September 1944. (RiP)*

The tensions between Sofia and Moscow grew not only because of the repeated incursions of the Black Sea Fleet into the Bulgarian territorial waters, but also because of several small-scale Soviet bombing raids against some towns in the central and northeastern part of the country. The Bulgarian Foreign Ministry, of course, protested, but Moscow refused to accept the charges and on 10 September 1941 it issued a general denial to all allegations of interference in Bulgarian affairs. Nevertheless, Stalin's ambitions knew no limits and the actual Soviet interference continued unabated.

## THE BULGARIAN ARMED FORCES

The Kingdom of Bulgaria was a faithful ally of the German Empire during the First World War and paid dearly for that. Following the collapse of the Central Powers, it was forced to sign a humiliating treaty in Neuilly-sur-Seine on 27 November 1919. The treaty called for Bulgaria to cede huge territories to the neighboring countries that had fought for the victorious Entente. Worse still for the Bulgarians, the country was prohibited to maintain a strong army and its forces were limited to 20,000 troops, 10,000 gendarmerie and 3,000 border guards. It was also not allowed to have tanks, aircraft, submarines and heavy artillery.

*Bulgarian airmen inspect a B-24 Liberator shot down in the vicinity of Sofia, 1944. (Bulgarian Military Photo Archive)*

When the Bulgarian people learned of the terms of the treaty, they were outraged. However, they were not in a position to do anything about them. The result was a terrible national catastrophe, as about 300,000 Bulgarians were forced to leave their homes in the ceded lands. It was only in July 1938 when another treaty – that of Thessaloniki between Bulgaria, Great Britain and France – finally abolished the Neuilly-sur-Seine limitations.

\* \* \*

The restoration of compulsory military service allowed the Bulgarian High Command to create four territorial armies, a decent air force and a small navy. A fifth territorial army command was set up in the newly-acquired Macedonia in 1941. Apart from that, in 1942-43 two so-called "occupational corps" were formed in those parts of southeastern Serbia and northern Greece that were occupied by Bulgaria, but were not placed under Bulgarian administration.

The Bulgarian forces were armed with vast variety of weapons. There were pre-war imports from various countries in western and central Europe, booty captured by the Germans during their Blitzkrieg campaigns, as well as German-made armaments.

By the spring of 1944 the Bulgarian General Staff had managed to create the following ground forces:

- Twenty one infantry divisions
- One cavalry division
- One armored brigade
- Two assault-gun detachments
- One airborne battalion

The infantry divisions were created in accordance with the pre-war concepts. They were large (13,000 to 14,000 men), infantry-heavy (three infantry regiments with nine battalions altogether) and lacked firepower. They were virtually defenseless against determined air and armored attacks. (In contrast, the late-war infantry divisions of the main belligerents were either organized in accordance with the "many weapons – few men" formula or were of the same size, but were simply armed to the teeth.) Worse still, the Bulgarian infantry divisions had very limited mobility: the combat troops were on foot, the supply services and most of the artillery were horse-drawn and the number of motor vehicles was quite low.

*The briefing of Bulgarian Stuka crews before a mission, autumn of 1944. (Bulgarian Military Photo Archive)*

Moreover, even divisions with the same structure were not always of the same quality. The strongest ones were those numbered 1 through 12 (i.e. the "regular" ones). The four divisions formed on the territory of "New Bulgaria" (the lands acquired in 1941)[83] were of variable quality, while those numbered 22 through 29[84] were fit only for occupational duties and because of that were stationed in Serbia and Greece.

Throughout most of the war the Bulgarian armies were trained to fight an Anglo-American landing in Greece or a Turkish offensive in eastern Thrace (or a combined Allied-Turkish invasion, which was considered a worst-case scenario.) The Bulgarian infantrymen might be brave soldiers, but their lack of firepower and modern training would have put them at a serious disadvantage in a ground war with the Allies.

\* \* \*

The best Bulgarian units, namely the fighter units, the close-support air force, the armored brigade, the assault-gun detachments, the parachute battalion, the anti-submarine chasers, had received German weapons and were trained by Wehrmacht instructors, either in the Third Reich or in their home bases.

Second Lieutenant Georgi Kusev, commander of an anti-tank platoon of the Armored Reconnaissance Battalion (of the Armored Brigade) recalls his training in Wünsdorf:

> We were sent into Germany for three months in the school for *Panzertruppen* in Wünsdorf. [*Panzertruppenschule II*]. They did train us, but when there were more serious lectures we were not allowed to go. Although we were allies, they were cautious.
> I was very impressed by the difference between the SS officers and the rest. There was a big difference in the self-confidence. There were many wounded military men from all ranks.
> They had large halls full with trophy armored fighting vehicles. We were most impressed by the Soviet heavy tanks. They had a T34 tank. The Germans confessed that they still weren't having much success creating an analogous design. They said that their tanks were using petrol since they did not have resources for the production of diesel.

*The crew of a Bulgarian Stuka board their plane before take-off, autumn of 1944. (Bulgarian Military Photo Archive)*

---

83  14th, 15th, 16th and 17th Infantry Divisions.
84  22nd, 24th, 25th, 27th, 28th and 29th Infantry Divisions.

Already back then we felt that the Germans were going to lose the war. There was deficit of everything in Berlin where we were based. There were a lot more goods in Bulgaria than in Germany.

In the training we learned a lot, but mostly about the tactics. We did not study German weapons. There was a clearly expressed distrust towards us.[85]

Overall, the German instructors had very little influence over the development of the armored brigade. Usually, they maintained contact with the battalion commanders and only occasionally with the company and platoon leaders. This is confirmed by one of Kusev's comrades, Second Lieutenant Georgi Georgiev, who was in charge with one of the brigade's armored car platoons:

There was a German instructor, a Major. He came from North Africa. He had participated in the battle of El Alamein. He had received severe burns and had not yet recovered. He attended silently the developments of our projects for action. We had very few conversations with him. Additionally, I did not speak German. He spoke mainly with the commanders of the Armored Car Company and the [Armored] Reconnaissance Battalion.

When we, the young officers from the Armored Car Company, were presented to the German Major, he smiled and said: "Do you know how big are the losses of the German armored car units from the beginning of the war till now?" And he gave us the answer himself – 300%.

I do not remember him saying anything concrete. He did not train us directly. He came to us time to time but this was not very often.[86]

# THE RED TIDE IS COMING

Save for some sporadic attacks, the Allied bombing offensive against Bulgaria largely ceased after 17 April 1944. This, however, had nothing to do with Filov's and Bozhilov's peace-negotiation efforts, but with the overall Anglo-American strategy. Rumania and Hungary were next in the list and the Liberators and Flying Fortresses were redirected there.

In May Bozhilov's government fell and Ivan Bagrayanov was named the new prime minister. In the meantime, the underground activity of the Soviet-sponsored Fatherland Front increased. Even though small in size (when compared to the neighboring Yugoslavia and Greece), the Bulgarian partisans conducted several daring raids against stores, installations and ground communications. Like Tito's movement, the Bulgarian communist partisans counted very much on weapons parachuted by the Allies or stolen from the army.

Hitler, in turn, was still not keen to give up Bulgaria. As it becomes clear from the minutes of his meeting with Jodl on 31 July, the country played a central part in his Balkan strategy:

But also in Bulgaria they're slowly coming to the idea: yes, if Germany collapses, then what? We small ones can't do it. If the big one can't do it, we can't do it. There's also something else that depends on the stabilization of the Eastern Front, in my view. In the end the attitude of all the small Balkan states depends on it: […] The second – just as important – is, of course, the attitude of Bulgaria. Because without Bulgaria it's practically impossible to secure the Balkan area so that we can get ore from Greece, etc. We need Bulgaria for that no matter what. Also in securing against bands, etc., we need Bulgaria. But it also depends partly on the fact that we really can stand in the East, and of course, that we don't have a crisis in the rear or in the heart of Europe.[87]

The collapse of the German front in Rumania led to the some of the most dramatic events in the Bulgarian history.

On 26 August Bagryanov's government declared Bulgaria's neutrality and the authorities began to intern the German troops fleeing from Rumania. The personnel of the German military missions and the Kriegsmarine were luckier, because they were allowed to cross the country in closed boxcars. The vessels, however, could not be spared and in late August several dozen ships and boats that had just escaped from the Constanța naval base were scuttled off the Bulgarian shore, not far from Varna and Burgas.

Simultaneously, the Bulgarian forces employed in the occupation of Serbia were ordered to return to the homeland. Their withdrawal, however, was only partially successful, because the Germans disarmed many of the units and even took some of them prisoner.

85   K. Matev, "The Armoured Forces of the Bulgarian Army 1936-45", Solihull, Helion & Company, 2015, p. 184.
86   Ibid., pp. 184-192.
87   Heiber and Glantz, op. cit., p. 448.

\* \* \*

The declared neutrality didn't calm the structures of the Fatherland Front. Just the contrary, on orders from Moscow its armed branch, the partisans became more active and even aggressive. The tensions within the country escalated and by 1 September Bagryanov and his government resigned. Konstantin Muraviev, an Anglophile and one of the most prominent leaders of the legal opposition within the Bulgarian parliament, was chosen his successor. On the same day some forward detachments of 3rd Ukrainian Front reached the northeastern Bulgarian-Rumanian border but were instructed to stop there and restrain themselves from crossing it.

Fearing the worst (a Soviet invasion) Muraviev immediately resumed the peace talks with the Allies. A special envoy, Moshanov, was urgently dispatched to Cairo

*A Soviet BA-64 armored car of 4th Guards Mechanized Corps enters a Bulgarian town, September 1944. (Bulgarian Military Photo Archive)*

with the mission to reach a truce with the Anti-Nazi Coalition. At the same time Muraviev also promised amnesty to all political prisoners, declared full support to democratic reforms abolished all laws against Jews.

In the meantime, Moshanov, who was already in Cairo, completely sabotaged the negotiations with the Allies, refusing to sign the documents offered to him. (There is strong evidence that he was actually Stalin's spy.) By doing so he not only betrayed his country and his government, but also opened the door for Soviet aggression.

Stalin didn't wait long. In the evening of 5 September, much to the shock of his Western Allies, the USSR declared war on the Bulgarian Kingdom. The official *casus belli* was "the ongoing support to Nazi Germany". (A typical Soviet false claim, as usual.)

The country was thrown into chaos. The communist-dominated Fatherland Front initiated a wave of strikes, several towns and villages were occupied by the partisans. On 8 September Muraviev's government declared war on Germany and its allies. A bizarre situation ensued in which Bulgaria found itself at war with almost the entire world: the entire Anti-Nazi coalition (including the three major powers – USA, Great Britain and USSR) and the leftovers of the Axis camp (Germany, Japan, Hungary, etc).

On the same day 3rd Ukrainian Front finally crossed the border, but stopped upon reaching the Ruse – Burgas line in the northeast of the country. This was done on purpose – to allow the Communists to overthrow the government with their own hands and by doing so to make their power official in the eyes of the world. The coup took place during the night of 8/9 September. All key buildings in Sofia (the Ministry of War, the National Radio, the National Bank, etc) were seized by the partisans and some troops that had decided to change sides. Kimon Georgiev, one of the Fatherland Front founders, was declared new prime minister.

59

\* \* \*

Tolbukhin's 3rd Ukrainian Front resumed its advance shortly after the faithful coup. The 37th Army and 4th Guards Mechanized Corps were stationed in the east of the country. The 57th Army began slowly to move through northern Bulgaria. A special task force was urgently dispatched for Sofia, because the new government was seriously concerned about a possible German attack from the west. The Soviets entered the capital on 15 September.

The Bolshevik invasion was marked by brutality and arrogance. Many Soviet troops were involved in outrageous criminal acts that later earned the Red servicemen a notorious reputation as burglars and rapists all over eastern and central Europe. Looting, alcohol abuse and even rapes were quite common. In some cases Bulgarian peasants were killed. Of course, the local administration occasionally protested but everything was in vain.

The leadership of 3rd Ukrainian Front attempted to prevent the sudden breakdown of military discipline by issuing a series of strict orders. But the senior officers themselves also showed little respect to Bulgarian property – at several places they ordered confiscation of horses, food stocks, etc; some of the fuel dumps and motor transport of the Royal Bulgarian Army were declared trophies and also were "acquired". For instance, several hundred of the newest, German-made Bulgarian military trucks changed owners and saw action in the Belgrade Operation as official inventory of 3rd Ukrainian Front.

In the meantime, Stalin's attention was preoccupied with the next portion of his grandiose plans. On 20 September he ordered 57th Army to move to the Bulgarian-Yugoslav border and assemble in the vicinity of Vidin, in the northwest of the country. From there it was to strike towards Belgrade. 37th Army, on the other hand, was directed to move southwards and prepare an offensive against the completely neutral Turkey.[88] It was to be spearheaded by the full-strength 2nd Guards Mechanized Corps, which was ordered to entrain for Bulgaria after a six-month-long period of rest and refit. The dictator's Bosporus dream, however, proved to be short-lived, because on 23 September the Foreign Office informed Moscow that in the forthcoming days and weeks British troops would land in Greece. Most probably, Stalin decided not to go ahead with the invasion because he was afraid that the presence of an Allied military contingent in a country neighboring to Turkey could cause problems with Churchill and this, in turn, might lead to problems with the Lend-lease supplies.

* * *

The Bulgarian hostilities with the Germans began immediately after the country's declaration of war on the Third Reich. On 9 September German troops attacked and disarmed the Bulgarian garrison in Skopje (14th Infantry Division). The other two divisions stationed in Macedonia (15th and 17th), however, managed to fight their way out. The Germans even took Kula – a small town in the northwest of the country – but decided to withdraw after less than a week.

In response to increasing danger from the west, the Fatherland Front government declared mobilization and brought most of the divisions to their full wartime strength. Three armies were positioned along the western border. The strongest of them was 2nd Army, which was placed to the west of Sofia. It consisted of six divisions plus the armored brigade. The other two armies – the 1st and the 4th – were mere corps. Each of them had just two divisions.

The Fatherland Front introduced some "innovations" to guarantee the loyalty of the troops to the new regime. For instance, Soviet-style "deputy commanders" (i.e. commissars) were established to control and improve the morale of the units. They were available at every level of command, down to company. Moreover, so-called "Guards" companies made of partisans (now dressed in army uniforms) were incorporated in every regiment to enhance the power of the deputy commanders. They acted as chain dogs of the communist party. Apart from that, before the beginning of the offensive operations all of the units and formations were purged of "suspicious elements", mostly officers, who had been involved in anti-partisan actions or were simply unsympathetic to the communist causes.

Needless to say, the new war was not popular among most of the troops. The soldiers and the officers didn't harbor hatred against their recent allies and simply lacked the basic motivation to fight them. Many servicemen couldn't figure out why they had to be part of this war. Another source of concern was the Soviet occupation – nearly everyone in uniform worried about the safety of their beloved ones at home.

In their operations against the Germans the Bulgarian forces had to cooperate with the Yugoslavian partisans on a territory now declared Yugoslavian. The distrust between the unlikely allies was mutual and this promised nothing but problems.

Fitzroy Maclean, the head of the British liaison mission to the HQ of the Yugoslav partisan army, recalls the mood in their camp when they heard the news:

Then almost immediately we hear that the Bulgars have entered the war on our side. There is a tendency to refer to them as Slav Brothers. But this goes against the grain with a good many people, for the atrocities committed by the Bulgars are still fresh in their minds. The Bulgars, for their part, do not seem to care very much which side they are on. Having hitherto fought for the Germans with efficiency and brutality, they now fight against them in exactly the same fashion, still wearing their German-type helmets and uniforms.[89]

88   *Stavka* directive # 220222. TsAMO, fu. 148a, inv. 3763, f. 167, p. 56. Reproduced in V. Zolotarev, *"Velikaia Otechestvennaia Voina"*, Vol. 16(5-4), Terra, Moscow, 1999, p. 148.

89   F. MacLean, "Eastern Approaches", London, Jonathan Cape, 1949, pp. 494-495.

# — CHAPTER 3 —

# THE SOUTHEAST

## THE BALKAN RESISTANCE MOVEMENTS

Hitler invaded the Balkans in April 1941 with the objective of securing his southern flank before the attack on the Soviet Union. The offensive was carried out in a true Blitzkrieg style and ended up in a spectacular victory.

The fate of the conquered states was grim. The Kingdom of Yugoslavia was dismembered. It was succeeded by a puppet Serbian republic and the "independent state" of Croatia. The rest of the former kingdom was ceded to its neighbors. Since neither the Serbian, nor the Croatian "governments" were able to maintain any semblance of order, large occupational forces from Germany, Italy and Bulgaria were moved into their territories.

The situation in Greece was no different. Part of its lands were returned to Bulgaria, while the bulk of the country was placed under Italian control. The Germans, however, remained in control of the key areas, such as Athens, Thessaloniki, Crete and some of Aegean islands. Like in Serbia, a collaborationist government was installed, but it had no real power.

\* \* \*

Few Serbians and Greeks actively cooperated with the occupiers. Most of them chose either to remain passive bystanders or to join the resistance. The latter began to take shape by the autumn of 1941. As in many other countries occupied by the Nazis, two rival movements came in to being: one inspired by the respective government in exile and one controlled by the local communist party. The latter usually were stronger and much more numerous. Before long the actions of the resistance movements evolved into a partisan war. But pretty often the rival parties fought with each other or separately attacked ethnic groups that were more sympathetic to the occupying regimes. That's why, in many respects what happened in the Balkans back then safely could be described as a series of civil wars.

The main resistance force in Greece was the National Liberation Front (EAM), an umbrella organization dominated by the local communists. Its military wing was called Greek People's Liberation Army (ELAS), which strength by September 1943 totaled about 15,000 fighters plus some 20,000 reserves. It gradually obtained Soviet support and by the end of the war its strength grew to an impressive 50,000.

The rival guerilla group was called the National Republican Greek League (EDES). It received extensive support from the British government, which hoped it would become a counterweight to ELAS. EDES operated mostly in the northwest of the country and its strength was about the half of the size of its communist counterpart.

Given their respective backgrounds, the conflict between ELAS and EDES was inevitable right from outset. ELAS, which had a clear superiority over its rivals in terms of numbers, organization and the size of territory controlled by its detachments, attempted with ruthless determination to annihilate their opponents. It safely can be said that throughout most of the occupation the Greek resistance movements clashed with each other nearly as often as they attacked the Axis forces.

Stalin did realize that he would not be able to take over Greece and therefore he decided to accept British proposal to divide the Balkans into respective spheres of influence. In July 1944 he traded Greece for Rumania. Thus ELAS were clearly abandoned to their fate and maybe even betrayed. What followed was a brutal civil war that lasted until the autumn of 1949.

\* \* \*

In Yugoslavia the situation with the resistant movements was a little bit different. Those who associated themselves with the government-in-exile were called Chetniks and at first indeed fought for the Allied cause. But from the autumn of 1941 their leader, Draža Mihailović, decided to go his own way and began to act rather as an independent warlord than as a head of a resistance movement. Pretty often the Chetniks, who generally identified themselves as royalists and nationalists, cooperated with the occupying German and Italian forces. They also used every opportunity to attack the other ethnic groups living then in Yugoslavia, especially the Croats, Bosnians and Albanians. But their main target remained the communists.

Even though at first glance the behavior of the Chetniks seems irrational and illogical, one must keep in mind that the Chetniks considered themselves, first and foremost, nationalists. They worshiped the "Greater Serbia" and truly believed that by carrying out ethnic cleansing actions in territories they considered rightfully and historically Serbian they were ensuring the safety of the domestic ethnic Serb populations. In this regard, their bloody conflict with the communist partisans is easy to understand, because Mihailović viewed the pan-ethnic policies proclaimed by them as totally anti-Serbian.

Initially, the Chetniks were actively assisted by the Allies, but when intelligence reports claiming that Mihailović had in several occasions cooperated with the occupiers reached the British and the Americans, Washington and London decided to shift their support to the more predictable communist partisan movement. By the beginning of 1944 the relations between Mihailović and the Allied liaisons de facto ceased.

The "other" resistance movement was led by the chairman of the Yugoslavian Communist Party, Josip Broz Tito. It was the military arm of the Unitary National Liberation Front (JNOF), a typical Balkan leftist umbrella organization that was officially represented by the Anti-Fascist Council for the National Liberation of Yugoslavia (AVNOJ). Throughout most of the

*Troops of 1. Mountain Division in action somewhere in Central Yugoslavia, late summer 1944. (NAC)*

62

conflict it was Serbian-dominated, even though Tito himself was of mixed Croatian/Slovene origin.

At first, the partisans were poorly armed, because their only source of weapons were the occupiers. But after the 1943 Tehran Conference, where they were officially recognized as the legitimate national liberation force by the Allies, the partisans received constantly increasing quantities of supplies from both the Western Allies and the Soviets, and even some close-air support. This allowed Tito to create a huge army that by the end of the war numbered about 800,000 fighters.

Here is the place to say, that AVNOJ was not very popular (or was totally unpopular) in certain areas where the Serbs were largely detested by the locals, because they were traditionally seen as oppressors. Not surprisingly, in Macedonia and Vojvodina (returned to Bulgaria and Hungary, respectively), as well as in Kosovo, by the beginning of 1944 there was still very little partisan activity. One of the reasons for that was definitely the fact that the communist partisans lacked their traditional

(Serbian) ethnic base, because most of the Serbian colonists that had been settled there after the Balkan and First World Wars were expelled by the new local administration. Tito had no other choice left, but to "import" partisan units in these lands from the neighboring regions.

\* \* \*

Typically for many authoritarian leaders, Tito held simultaneously several posts - General Secretary of the Communist Party of Yugoslavia, President of the National Committee of Liberation and Supreme Commander of the AVNOJ. And because of the latter, on 29 November 1943 the rank of "Marshal of Yugoslavia" at the second session of AVNOJ, even though his own military education was limited to the one received in the school for non-commissioned officers of the Austro-Hungarian Army in Budapest on the eve of the First World War, after which he was promoted to sergeant-major.

Tito's primary objective was to create a federal multi-ethnic communist state in Yugoslavia. The propaganda structures of the CPY used this and attempted to appeal to all ethnic groups within the kingdom, claiming that they would preserve the rights of each these groups. In some respects, however, the Marshal was no different from the royalist rulers who dreamed of "Great Serbia". By the war's end, he intended to create a mini-communist empire in the southeast of Europe that would "swallow" the entire Bulgaria and Albania, as well as would acquire certain territories from the other neighboring countries like Greece, Rumania, Hungary, Austria and Italy.

The only Yugoslavian Marshal resembled Stalin not only in territorial ambitions, but also in other respects. In May 1944, he founded an intelligence service known as OZNA (the Serbian abbreviation of the Department for People's Protection) that was modeled after the notorious Soviet NKVD. It combined both a military intelligence service and a political secret police of the Communist Party of Yugoslavia. Furthermore, in August 1944 Tito established a special army unit called KNOJ (Korpus narodne odbrane Jugoslavije - People's Defense Force of Yugoslavia), which chief function was the physical elimination of Chetniks, Croatian Ustaša and other ideological enemies.

Tito showed his true face of a brutal communist warlord already in the autumn of 1943 when he sanctioned the mass killings of Istrian Italians. It was followed by a wave of purges in Serbia (and especially in Vojvodina) in late 1944, shortly after the communist authorities gained control over the country. Their main targets were the ethnic Hungarians and Germans, as well as many Serbs accused of collaboration.

*The photo clearly shows the hardships experienced by the German troops retreating from the southern and central Balkans in the autumn of 1944. (NAC)*

*A German Sd.Kfz.233 eight-wheeled heavy armored car on a patrol mission in Yugoslavia, December 1943. (NAC)*

*StuG IV assault guns of 4. SS-Polizei-Panzer-Grenadier-Division in Thessaloniki, April 1944. (NAC)*

The death toll amounted to tens of thousands. The Bulgarians (in Macedonia) and Albanians (in Kosovo) who were not sympathetic to the new regime were also not spared. But the culmination of this Red terror (fueled by revenge, but probably also by some other, more rational considerations) was definitely the series of mass killings that occurred in the northwestern Yugoslavian borderlands right after the war's end. Their victims were many thousands of Croats, Serbs, Slovenes, Montenegrins, Russians and Germans, both POWs and civilian refugees.

* * *

In June 1944 Tito established his main HQ on the island of Vis, not far from the Croatian coast, which already had been liberated by the Royal Navy. This allowed him not only to conduct the military operations from a safe place, but also to make his power official. In early August he met with Churchill in Rome. On 14 August an agreement was signed on the island between Partisans and the Government in exile (the so-called Tito-Šubašić agreement), which was an attempt by the Western Allies to merge the Royal Yugoslavian government-in-exile with the communist-led resistance. The document in question called on all Serbs, Croats and Slovenes to join the partisans. In so doing the AVNOJ became the official Yugoslav Allied force. Consequently, on 29 August King Peter II dismissed Draža Mihailović as Chief-of-Staff of the (Royal) Yugoslav Army and on 12 September appointed Tito in his place. A week later he was flown out from Vis in complete secrecy by a Soviet plane, literally under the nose of the British military mission, because Stalin wanted to negotiate the entry of the Red Army in Yugoslavia *tête-à-tête* with the communist warlord, as well as to probe the loyalty of the latter.

The talks didn't last long and the two communist leaders quickly reached a full agreement on joint actions on Yugoslavian territory. Both Stalin and Tito were definitely very pleased by the developments. The former got the chance to expand his influence further to the southwest, as well as was to secure a quick passage for 3rd Ukrainian Front to Hungary. The latter viewed the arrival of the Red Army (though with some caution) as a sure way to fortify and legitimize his power.

With two Soviet Fronts deploying along the eastern and northeastern borders of prewar Yugoslavia, Tito was now ready to strike and grab the power in Belgrade. He was quite confident, because he had a substantial force totaling up to 400,000 fighters at his disposal. It was made of about fifty divisions plus several independent brigades and detachments. But it was no longer made of highly motivated volunteers

only. The clearing of a considerable part of Yugoslavian territories allowed Tito to launch a conscription campaign, forcing civilians in certain areas to join the military. The troops already wore uniforms and had a clearly visible structure. But in many other respects the AVNOJ army retained its partisan character. It was insufficiently trained and armed, lacked heavy weapons and the basic transportation means, and the tactical cooperation between the branches was almost non-existent. On the top of that, the so-called divisions were quite small in size and poorly disciplined.

By the end of September the bulk of Tito's partisan army had already been regrouped to central Serbia. It was positioned along the main communication lines of the German troops, as well as in the vicinity of the key settlements. Tito himself didn't return to Vis, but moved his HQ to Craiova, the biggest town in southwestern Rumania, which was situated about 350 km to the east of Belgrade

## THE AXIS OCCUPATION

During the first two years of the Axis occupation of the Balkans the Germans maintained a relatively small force on the peninsula. It was Italy that until August 1943 held the most territory. Its zones of occupation included the western part of Croatia, Montenegro, an enhanced version of Albania (with Kosovo) and about 70% of Greece. Germany controlled northern Slovenia, Serbia, the Macedonian territory around Salonika, a strip of Greek land on the Turkish border, the Piraeus, most of the islands in the Aegean Sea, including Crete.

Hitler's other allies also participated in the occupation. As it was already mentioned, Bulgaria got western Thrace and Yugoslavian Macedonia, and provided troops for securing of central and southern Serbia. Hungary and Rumania each took a piece of the dismembered Yugoslavia north of the Danube (Vojvodina and Banat, respectively). The "Independent State" of Croatia, including the entire Bosnia and Hercegovina, was in fact a territorial condominium of Germany and Italy. Its leader, Dr. Ante Pavelić and his Ustaši Movement were not strong enough to provide security for the entire country, that's why the presence of the German and Italian troops was very much needed. After Italy surrendered in September 1943, Germany took over all Italian zones. The Bulgarian area in northern Greece was slightly enlarged and puppet governments were established in the former Italian territories Albania and Montenegro.

*Vehicles of 7. SS-Mountain Division "Prinz Eugen" during their transfer to Eastern Serbia, ca. September 1944. (NAC)*

***

The surrender of Italy placed a heavy burden on the shoulders of the Third Reich and the Wehrmacht, because it vastly increased the German military and administrative responsibilities. Even though by the end of 1943 the number of the German divisions in the Balkans increased to 18, the troop requirements could only be partly met, and nearly everywhere Hitler had to depend on collaborator units.

The theater command was organized in somewhat strange manner. The Fuhrer appointed *Feldmarschall* Maximilian von Weichs as Commander-in-Chief Southeast (*Oberbefehlshaber Südost*), and at the same time named him commander of Army Group "F". In his first function Weichs was the supreme commander of the entire theater; in the second he had operational leadership of the troops in most of Yugoslavia (save for Macedonia) and Albania. To oversee the coastal defense on the Adriatic, where an Allied landing was expected, in the summer of 1943 he was given the headquarters of 2. Panzer-Army. Operational command in mainland Greece and on the Aegean islands went to Army Group "E" of Generaloberst Alexander Löhr. Apart from that, von Weichs had to fulfill administrative and diplomatic functions, because he was tasked with territorial responsibility for military government and relations with the governments of the satellite and puppet states.

The Commander-in-Chief Southeast had two main military missions:

- To defend the coasts of the Balkan Peninsula and
- To combat the resistance movements in the interior.

Due to the rugged, mountainous terrain and because the Wehrmacht could not afford to keep the equipment and vehicles required for mobile forces in such an inactive theater of war, the coastal defense was predominately static. This forced von Weichs to spread his strength thinly over a very vast area. Some of his best formations, namely 4. SS-Polizei-Panzer-Grenadier-Division, 22. Infantry Division and Assault Division "Rhodes" - were kept where the Allied invasion was most likely to occur: in the south of Greece, on Crete and the Dodecanese Islands in the southeastern Aegean. Save for the SS-division, by the spring of 1944 the rest were completely immobile and could be reached only by air or by small vessels.

The rest of the forces were a mixed bag. The strongest of them, without doubt, were the two mountain divisions (1. and 7. SS "*Prinz Eugen*"), as well as the "Brandenburg" Division, which

*Soldiers of 7. SS-Mountain Division "Prinz Eugen" talk to local Muslims somewhere in Central Yugoslavia, late summer 1944. (NAC)*

regiments were spread all over the entire region. The infantry divisions were rather second-rate and lacked any frontline experience. The same applies to the Jaeger divisions, which were created with anti-guerilla warfare in mind. Apart from that, there was also a considerable number of smaller units – regiments, battalions, etc. - fit only for occupational service. If there was something common between the forces under von Weichs, it was that all of them were equipped and armed to considerable degree with Italian-manufactured heavy weapons and other materiel that had been confiscated from their former allies after their ill-fated attempt to surrender in September 1943.

*Generaloberst Alexander Löhr, the Commander-in-Chief of Army Group "E". (NARA)*

Von Weichs had very few armored vehicles at his disposal and many of them were already obsolete. Worse still, since the Luftwaffe was actively engaged on the main fronts, the Axis troops deployed in the Balkans were de facto deprived of close-air support. (The German air units totaled several dozens of Fw 190s fighter-bombers plus some obsolete biplanes.)

The anti-partisan actions carried on by both von Weichs and Löhr were usually brutal and ferocious. Many civilians were shot in reprisal or were killed with no reason; their houses were burned to the ground. But these savage methods could not pacify the rebellious

areas. By September 1944 only the main settlements and their vicinity were still in German hands. The occupiers supplied their garrisons only with great difficulty, because their ground communications were time and again attacked by partisans and saboteurs.

The forces that Commander-in-Chief Southeast could spare for the war against the partisans were always insufficient to conduct full-scale operations. The situation could be even worse, but the Axis occupying forces frequently benefited from conflicts between the various resistance movements.

\* \* \*

Hitler wanted to hold the Balkans, because, in his opinion the southeastern theater of war was threatening the Allied sea lanes in the eastern Mediterranean and also was acting as a counterweight to the Allied pressure on neutral Turkey. Even though by mid-1944 this strategy was no longer making any sense, the Führer still believed that the stubborn defense of the peninsula was the only way to keep Turkey neutral and retain Bulgaria, Rumania, and Hungary in the Axis camp. On 31 July 1944, when Turkey was about to break diplomatic relations with the Third Reich, Hitler said the following:

> In my opinion, we will also be able to fix the thing in the East. The great concern I see is obviously the Balkans. I have the fundamental conviction: if today the Turks were persuaded – like the Finns – that we can hold out, then they wouldn't lift a finger. Everyone has only the one concern that they might sit on the ground between all the chairs. That's their concern. So if we manage through some act of extremely decisive resistance or even a successful big battle somewhere, if we manage to regain the trust of those people – the trust that we can hold this, and that this withdrawal is only in the end to shorten the front, because otherwise we couldn't do it on all fronts – then I'm convinced that we could bring the Turks to a more-or-less waiting attitude, even though they severed the relationships themselves.[90]

As result of Hitler's insane obsession "to hold everywhere", the forces of yet another theater of war were tied down without being even involved in active regular combat.

69

90   Heiber and Glantz, op. cit., p. 448.

The fact that von Weichs' best forces were looking seaward when the deadliest threat was looming behind their backs, made the whole situation even more ridiculous.

# THE WITHDRAWAL

The surrender of Rumania, coupled with the collapse of the entire Army Group "South Ukraine", and the neutrality declared by Bulgaria in late August 1944 forced Hitler to accept the truth that certain areas of the Balkans could no longer be held. That's why already on 23 August he sanctioned a gradual evacuation from southern Greece. The weight of the defense had to be moved north, into Yugoslavia, with the intention of deploying the main body of Army Group "E" along the Athens-Thessaloniki-Belgrade railway.

The withdrawal promised to be difficult. On paper the ration strength of Commander-in-Chief Southeast was up to 900,000, but this included a large portion of non-combat personnel (technicians, auxiliaries, civilian helpers, foreign volunteers, etc.), as well as the occupational divisions of the still allied Bulgaria. The actual combat strength of von Weichs' forces was perhaps no more than 600,000. About half of them (up to 300,000) were in Greece with Army Group "E", of which ca. 90,000 were garrisoning the Aegean islands. Even though

*SS-Oberführer Otto Kumm, (shown here as an SS-Standartenführer) the commander of 7. SS-Mountain Division "Prinz Eugen". (NARA)*

some of these troops were by no means first class (for instance, the so called "fortress" battalions that were made of over-age and partially fit for service men), all of them were in possession of huge quantities of various materiel, as well as of food-stores that had to be either evacuated or destroyed. The rapid evacuation from the islands would require naval resources that the Kriegsmarine was not able to provide, let alone that the lines of communication in Greece and Yugoslavia were sparse and primitive.

The overall attitude of the Bulgarians caused worries, too. Von Weichs had every reason to believe that they would defect and because of that on 26 August he instructed 1. Mountain Division to move out of Greece and assemble in southern Serbia, just to the north of the Bulgarian occupation zone. On 30 August, when it was already clear that Bulgaria would quit the Axis alliance in a matter of days, he directed the mountain division to deploy at Niš, while 7. SS-Mountain Division "*Prinz Eugen*" and 11. Luftwaffe Field Division were told to move into the Bulgarian-held Macedonia and hold the road and rail junction at Skopje. The 4. SS-Polizei-Panzer-Grenadier-Division, in transit from Greece, was also instructed to intervene. By doing so, von Weichs managed to forestall the events that lied ahead and set up a protective belt that would screen the main retreat route.

\* \* \*

On 29 August the OKW issued an "Order for the Defense of the Southeast", which directed von Weichs to deploy his reserves in the Thessaloniki-Niš-Belgrade area and to begin the withdrawal of Army Group "E" from southern Greece to the line [Island of] Corfu-Mount Olympus.

In the meantime the situation grew worse for the Germans. On 8 September the USSR declared war on Bulgaria and 3rd Ukrainian Front began to pour into the country from the northeast. Bulgaria, which was already at war with Germany, offered no resistance to the invaders and surrendered on the same day. The Germans reacted immediately and already on 9 September attacked the garrisons of their former ally in Macedonia. Some of them offered stiff resistance and managed to break out, but the one in the main city, Skopje, surrendered without a fight. Meanwhile, the Bulgarian occupational corps in Serbia was disarmed and partially taken prisoner. Before long the vital retreat route of Army Group "E" from Greece – i.e. the Thessaloniki-Niš-Belgrade motorway and railroad – was firmly in German hands.

The most difficult part proved to be getting the troops off the Aegean islands. They were evacuated both by sea and by air, facing increasing opposition from the

70

Allied air force and the Royal Navy. At first, the 15th Air Force bombed predominately the railways in Yugoslavia, leading to Belgrade, but in mid-September the British and American bombers raided the airfields in the vicinity of Athens, inflicting heavy damage on the Ju 52 transport aircraft stationed there. But this was not all. During the next few days British ships, including aircraft carriers with night fighters, were moved into the Aegean Sea and began mercilessly to hunt the German ships and planes engaged in evacuation of the islands.

By some miracle most of the combat worthy elements were evacuated to the continent. By the end of October 1944, when the operation ceased completely, the Kriegsmarine succeeded in bringing to the mainland more than 37,000 troops; another 30,000 were flown out by transport planes. More than 23,000 Germans and about 10,000 Italians, however, had to be left behind. They remained there till the end of the war, holding out in Crete and the Dodecanese Islands.

\* \* \*

The withdrawal of Army Group "E" to the north was not only long but was difficult as well. There were very few railways and most of the German units were forced to retreat along dusty side roads, sneaking through the valleys and endless ravines of Greece, Albania, Macedonia and Serbia. On their way they were repeatedly harassed by local partisans. One of the German combatants recalls the retreat as "a terrible affair":

> The roads would be mined sometimes in the passes, for twenty or thirty kilometers at a stretch, and after the first week we had lost most of our vehicles. Many of the men had worn out their shoes and discarded everything except their rifles. At night we had to mount half the company on guard for the partisans would allow us no rest. Every village that we passed through bore testimony to the unbelievable ferocity of the partisan warfare...[91]

The relatively timely and successful withdrawal of the army group from Greece allowed von Weichs by the end of September 1944 to establish a relatively stable and continuous defensive line running along the prewar Bulgarian-Yugoslavian border. In doing this he was unexpectedly helped by the Soviets themselves who considerably delayed their advance through Bulgaria.

91    A. Clark, "Barbarossa", New York, Morrow, 1985, p. 406.

\* \* \*

The German forces opposing Tolbukhin had only one mission – to safeguard the retreat of the main body of Army Group "E" from Greece. For that purpose by the end of September they were placed under the unified command of *General der Infanterie* Hans Felber and his Army Detachment "Serbia" (*Armeeabteilung Serbien*).

The order of battle of the army detachment was typical for many other German late-war combat formations. Nominally, it was made of four divisions, but in reality it consisted of many battle groups of various sizes and combat worth. Among them, for instance, there was an SS mountain division comprising ethnic Germans from Yugoslavia and Rumania, a Russian volunteer security corps, SS police units, an ad-hoc infantry battalion constituted of sailors and so on. It is important to note that a considerable part of the weapons and equipment used by Felber's men was booty captured during the campaigns in the west, east and south.

Felber's frontage was divided into two clearly visible sectors separated by the Danube. The one to the north of the river, in the southern Banat, was assigned to *General der Infanterie* Wilhelm Schneckenburger, a Knight's Cross holder and an experienced Eastern Front veteran. He fulfilled the role of a corps commander, but his ad-hoc corps (*Gruppe General Schneckenburger*) had quite insignificant forces in his order of battle: the motorized Grenadier-Brigade 92 and some smaller units.

To the south of the Danube operated another makeshift corps – that of *General der Infanterie* Friedrich-Wilhelm Müller, a highly decorated and brutal officer, who was very familiar with the Balkan theater of war. Müller's group (*Gruppe General Müller*) was much stronger, but at the same time he held a much wider sector, which southern flank was stretched as far as the western approaches to Sofia.

Von Weichs was well aware that forming a continuous defensive line with these insignificant forces was out of question. That's why he focused his efforts on holding the key junctions – towns, villages, mountain passes – where strongpoints were set up in a hurry. Special attention was paid to the Thessaloniki - Belgrade railway, which was crucial as an escape corridor for the German military forces retreating from Greece. Not surprisingly, all available tactical reserves were employed to protect the vital railroad. These included the best divisions von Weichs had at his disposal. They were divided between both army groups.

Upon retaking Macedonia from the Bulgarians, Army Group "E" formed a blocking force there, which official designation was *Wehrmachtbefehlshaber Mazedonien* (Military Commander "Macedonia"). This makeshift corps consisted of two divisions

– the elite 22. Infantry Division, which had been urgently flown out from Crete, and 11. Luftwaffe Field Division, which had been transferred from the vicinity of Athens. Divisions like the latter were usually considered combat unworthy, but this particular one was still good for the Balkan theater of war.

Two of the best divisions of Army Group "F" – 1. Mountain Division and 7. SS-Mountain Division *"Prinz Eugen"* - were transferred in the first days of September 1944 from Central Yugoslavia/Montenegro (as usual, in a great hurry) to the northwestern border of Bulgaria. The former was considered a truly elite formation, perfectly suited for warfare in rugged terrain. The latter was a typical SS division, which was made

*Feldmarschall Maximillian von Weichs, the Commander-in-Chief Southeast. (NARA)*

predominantly of *Volksdeutsche* (ethnic Germans), both volunteers and conscripts, from the Banat, Croatia, Hungary and Rumanian Transylvania. It was numerically super-strong (up to 20,000) and even had its own armored detachment. Both divisions were placed under Müller's *ad-hoc* corps.

The other units worth mentioning were two "Brandenburg" Regiments (1. and 2.), Grenadier-Brigade 92, Assault-Gun Brigades 191 and 201, two panzer battalions (12 and 202) and the Russian Security Corps. The "Brandenburg" regiments were considered elite, because they contained a large portion of commandos trained for special operations. (Usually, they were foreign German nationals who were convinced Nazi volunteers.) During the battle of Belgrade the Brandenburgers were split into battalions that were employed in a "fire-brigade" role all over central and northern Serbia. The panzer battalions were not fit for frontline combat, because they were outfitted with captured Italian and French tanks that were both obsolete and not

very reliable. The assault-gun brigades, on the other hand, were equipped with latest models StuG III/StuH assault guns and howitzers. Grenadier-Brigade 92 was also a reliable formation, but it was given the impossible task to contain literally alone the drive of the Soviet 46th Army through the southern Banat.

The forces employed by Von Weichs could have been much stronger, but by mid-September 1944 he was ordered to release his sole armored formation, 4. SS-Polizei-Panzer-Grenadier Division. It was transferred to the north, in the vicinity of the Rumanian town of Timişoara, to plug the gap between the Army Groups "South Ukraine" and "F".

## THE SOVIET AIR STRIKES

The first Soviet formation that went into action against the German forces still occupying the western and southern parts of the Balkans was 17th Air Army. From 15 to 17 September its units relocated to three major airfields in the immediate vicinity of Sofia and wasting no time began pounding the German columns withdrawing from Greece. The Yaks, Shturmoviks and Bostons flew a number of 'free-hunt' missions against the enemy traffic in the areas of Skopje, Veles, Kraljevo and Niš. The strafing and bombing of the trains and truck columns continued day and night for exactly a week.[92]

Apart from that, 9-18-plane groups of Boston Mk. III bombers attacked the marshaling yards in Thessaloniki, Skopje, Kraljevo and Niš, where large numbers of trains were lined up like sitting ducks. But the seemingly easy tasks quickly developed into deadly nightmares, since the stations and the marshaling yards were protected by 15-16 light and heavy Flak batteries each. Even though some of the crews scored direct hits, and several big fires and explosions were reported, this came at a cost – two 'Bostons' were shot down over the target areas, while more than 50 others were damaged by splinters.[93]

Interestingly enough, the Soviet pilots met no opposition in the air. Whether because the Luftwaffe was "demoralized" (as Sudets' staff claimed) or because there were no German combat air units stationed in the area, but throughout the entire

92   TsAMO, fu. 370, inv. 6518, f. 201, pp. 38-39.
93   War diary of 244th Bomber Air Division. Entries for 17-22.9.1944. TsAMO, fu. 20224, inv. 1, f. 33, pp. 94-100.

Belgrade Operation the Red pilots felt complete masters of the sky. The same applied to the troops on the ground.

Stalin, who monitored with great interest the air raids of Sudets' army, eventually became very dissatisfied by the results reported to him. Fearing that the air strikes would lead to nothing but unjustified losses, and mechanical wear and tear, on 21 September the dictator ordered 17th Air Army to cease all further actions against the German ground communications.

## CLAIMS OF 17TH AIR ARMY (DAMAGE DONE TO THE ENEMY), 15 – 22 SEPTEMBER 1944

### Weapons, Equipment and Facilities Destroyed
- 11 aircraft
- 20 locomotives
- 15 railway trains
- 132 boxcars
- 1 fuel dump
- 1 ammunition dump
- 5 hangars
- 97 motor vehicles
- 38 horse-drawn carts
- 1 tank

### Damaged
- 4 railway bridges
- 1 tunnel

### Other
- 8 Flak batteries were silenced
- Up to 105 Axis troops were scattered and partially destroyed[94]

Whether because the Royal Bulgarian Air Force did have some dive bombers or because its pilots were far more familiar with the area, but their sole mission against the German railway traffic turned to be quite successful. On 20 September Bulgarian Stukas attacked trains carrying elements of 4. SS-Polizei-Panzer-Grenadier Division at the Gevgelija station, near today's Greek-Macedonian border.

The first wave consisted of 7 Ju 87s and 4 D520s, which struck the train station in the morning. Later on, another group appeared, this time with 20 Ju 87s and 10 Bf 109s. Even though they encountered heavy (8.8 cm) and light (2 cm/3,7 cm) Flak over the target area, the Stukas scored a lot of direct hits. Luckily for the Bulgarians, the Ju 87s carried 50 and 100 kg high explosive bombs that proved to be very effective against the AFVs of the SS division loaded on railway flatcars.

2nd Lieutenant Petko Nikolov was one of the Stuka pilots who participated in the very successful raid on the Gevgelija station. He was part of the second wave of 20 Ju 87s, which involved the entire dive-bomber wing. Nikolov recalls:

It was a very long train just exiting Gevgeli [Gevgelija] railway terminal, with two locomotives in the front of it and another one at the rear. Major Stefan Drumchev, CO of 1/2 *Orlyak* [wing], ordered the first *yato* [squadron] to attack the moving train, a bridge in front of it and a heavy-calibre AAA battery stationed next to the bridge. The rest of the aircrews were ordered to attack the main target. When over the moving train, the leader entered into a dive and I followed him in the attack as I was No 2 of the three aircraft. The train moved at a high speed and I looked at it to see the hits of the bombs dropped by the leader. In the first moment it looked like the bombs would enter directly into locomotive's chimney, but the hits were just in front of it, between 2 to 3m away. Suddenly everything went wrong for the train. As it hit the bomb pit, the second locomotive went on top of it and the cars got stacked in a zigzag pattern alongside the tracks. It was the last scene I saw while aiming at the third car just before dropping my bombs. When I was pulling out of the dive, I turned my head to look rearwards to observe the effect of the bomb hits. The third and fourth cars were in an overturned position, with fragments of these still flying in the air. After dropping the bombs, the aircraft joined in a circuit pattern next to the train, waiting for the last '*Shtuka*' to deliver its bomb load before mounting strafing passes, one by one, to further harass the train. Meanwhile, another flight managed to knock out the bridge and suppress the AAA battery.[95]

73

---

94    TsAMO, fu. 370, inv. 6518, f. 201, pp. 38-39.

95    A. Mladenov, E. Andonov and K. Grozev, "The Bulgarian Air Force in the Second World War", Solihull, Helion & Company, 2018, p. 103.

# CHAPTER 4

# THE BELGRADE OPERATION

## THE SOVIET OFFENSIVE PREPARATIONS

Tolbukhin used the operational pause to reorganize and resupply his forces, as well as to train the recently mobilized soldiers from Bessarabia and the Ukraine. The troops were issued with new weapons, vehicles, ammunition, fuel and signal equipment, thus ensuring that they would be brought to the highest level of combat readiness possible.[96]

It is worth mentioning that at that moment 3rd Ukrainian Front was perhaps the smallest Soviet army group engaged in the war against Nazi Germany. It was made of just two armies, one of which (the 37th) was deployed against Turkey, a mechanized (armored) corps, an air army and the Danube Flotilla. Apart from them, three were Bulgarian armies and several Yugoslavian partisan divisions, whose combat worth varied from average to poor.

The total strength of the Soviet, Bulgarian and Yugoslavian forces meant to participate in the Belgrade Operation amounted to about 660,000 men, 4,477 guns and mortars, 421 tanks and self-propelled guns, and 1,250 aircraft. It was estimated that Tolbukhin's formations had a superiority in men 4,4:1, two-fold superiority in artillery and 3,4:1 in armor.[97]

\* \* \*

During the preparation phase, special attention was paid to the so-called "party-political work", which was conducted in all military units. The main focus of the indoctrination carried out by the political officers was to strengthen the morale of the combatants and prepare them for the difficult fighting in the mountains of Serbia. The public lectures held by them, as well as several articles ran by the army and Front newspapers, emphasized the heroic struggle of the Yugoslavian people against the Axis occupiers and their friendly feelings towards the Soviet Union and the Red Army, in particular.[98] There is no doubt that the latter was done on purpose – given the fact that in southeastern Rumania and in Bulgaria the Red servicemen already had committed a number of outrageous acts of robbery, violence and rape, Tolbukhin and his staff had every reason to worry that the repetition of this criminal behavior might further discredit the new regimes, the Soviet state and the Communist ideology, in particular.

On the whole, in the autumn of 1944 the morale of the victorious Tolbukhin's troops was at its highest. Not surprisingly, in September and October of that year 10,443 officers and enlisted men of 3rd Ukrainian Front became members of the Communist Party.[99] However, it is difficult to say whether the increased share of communists within the combat formations had a direct relation to their performance on the battlefield.

---

96   "Istoria na Vtorata Svetovna Voina 1939 - 1945", Vol. 9, Sofia, Voenno izdatelstvo, 1980, p. 198.
97   "Istoria na Vtorata Svetovna Voina 1939 - 1945", op. cit., p. 199.
98   "Istoria na Vtorata Svetovna Voina 1939 - 1945", op. cit., pp. 198-199.
99   Ibid., p. 199.

*A Soviet sniper in action during the Belgrade Operation, September/October 1944. (RiP)*

\* \* \*

The planning of the offensive was yet to be completed when the Belgrade Operation began. Nevertheless, it was clear that the main blow would to be delivered by 57th Army, which was below average size for a late-war Soviet all-arms Army – just two rifle corps with six divisions between them. (A third rifle corps,[100] with three divisions, was added to the army's order of battle by the end of September.) It was led by Lieutenant-General Nikolai Gagen who was of German origin. Gagen's army was to receive support from its neighbors to the left and right, respectively, the three Bulgarian armies and the left flank of 2nd Ukrainian Front. Upon punching a hole in the German defense, a powerful exploitation force – 4th Guards Mechanized Corps - was to be unleashed with the task to lead the way as far as Belgrade.

Colonel-General Shtemenko, then the head of Operations Department of the Soviet General Staff, sheds more light on the planning of the Belgrade Operation:

The agreement of joint operations by the Soviet forces and the ANVOJ Army, which was reached in September 1944, was for the General Staff a very important document. It was the point of departure for planning military operations, with special attention devoted to Serbia, of course. We Soviet General Staff officers stubbornly looked for – and found – some vulnerable points in the defenses of Army Group F and proposed to exploit them to the fullest.

It was observed that Von Weichs had endeavored to organize his strongest defense line along the mountain ridges on the boundary between Serbia and Rumania. Here he had put up engineering structures that were both strong and deeply dug in, and had reinforced the troops of Army Group Serbia. On this sector of the front, the enemy's troop strength and resources were considerable. But along the Bulgarian border, toward which the main forces of Tolbukhin's front were advancing, the enemy had not provided a compact grouping of forces or a compact system of defenses. The Nazi command had not figured that the Red Army would get there that quickly, and it had counted too heavily on the mountainous terrain. And by the time we reached the Yugoslav border, Von Weichs had neither the time nor the means to take counteraction.

Running parallel to the Danube as it did, the German defense line struck us as a convenient objective for simultaneous strike along the whole front. The enemy was entrenched in the mountains. But he had no great reserves; and in the event of a threatened break-through he would either have to withdraw his garrisons to the interior, form them into concentrated forces, and throw them into a counterattack, or else use troops from the defensive lines for this purpose. Thus our task was to see to it that the line of pressure points against the enemy was stretched out as far as possible. Owing to Bulgaria's declaration of war against Germany, considerable Bulgarian forces could be used for this purpose – troops that knew how to operate in the mountains. In the sector of the main attack, of course, we had to use a great concentration of power and the great mobility of the experienced forces of the 3rd Ukrainian Front. They were in position to break through Army Group F's defenses at their strongest point, and to rapidly destroy the enemy's basic grouping, which would have an immediate effect on the over-all success of the three armies operating in concert.

The forces of the ANVOJ Army and the Bulgarian Army were to deal the enemy a staggering blow, to decoy a good part of his forces, tie them hand and foot, and make it impossible for the Nazis to create reserves. The Yugoslav and Bulgarian forces would have an especially difficult task if the enemy pulled his main forces

100  75th Rifle Corps.

out of Greece and sent them north. In that case they would have to take some heavy blows from the enemy, hold the line, and assure the actions of the Red Army. Such were some of the General Staff's ideas while the operations were being planned.[101]

*Soviet advance through open terrain during the Belgrade Operation, October 1944. (RiP)*

## 76  THE ATTACK

While the troops of 57th Army were still arriving in their final assembly area in northwestern Bulgaria, an unexpected crisis developed in the sector of its right-hand neighbor, the independent 75th Rifle Corps of 2nd Ukrainian Front. On 26 September a strong German battle group (1. Mountain Division reinforced with 2. Regiment "Brandenburg") struck the bridgehead held by the corps in the vicinity of Turnu Severin and threatened it with annihilation. In an attempt to help the hardly pressed neighbor, Tolbukhin ordered 57th Army to go over to the offensive literally from the march. Thus began the Belgrade Operation. What happened next was

quite unusual in the history of warfare. The initial advance developed into pursuit, the pursuit became a full-scale offensive, which culminated in the taking of the Yugoslavian capital. And all this occurred without any detailed battle plan (it was yet to be finished) and with an army that was still not fully deployed.

The Soviets immediately altered the situation in their favor. On 28 September the Stavka placed 75th Rifle Corps under 57th Army, thus considerably extending the frontline of the latter. Now Tolbukhin was in position to outflank the German "bulge" at Turnu Severin simultaneously from north and south and the Soviet Supreme Command ordered the Marshal to do exactly that. His new assignment was to destroy the enemy forces holding the Danube bend and secure the entire area between Donji Milanovac and Zaječar.

\* \* \*

The offensive of 57th Army was unleashed in the early hours of 28 September, when the forward detachment of 113th Rifle Division (a rifle regiment reinforced with the divisional anti-tank artillery battalion) advanced from the vicinity of Bregovo. It quickly crossed the Bulgarian-Yugoslavian border, then forced the River Timok and approached the town of Negotin, a major stronghold and the cornerstone of the German defense in that area. The few German machinegun nests encountered in the path of the detachment were silenced without delay by the accompanying guns.[102]

The detachment fully justified its purpose – to breach the enemy defensive line, thereby opening a gap through which the main exploitation forces would follow. In that particular case, it was the main body of 113th Rifle Division that was meant to exploit the initial success and maintain the offensive momentum. Already in the morning it hurriedly left its quarters accompanied by a powerful cluster of GHQ close-support combat units and rushed northwestwards.[103] On their way to their initial objective (Negotin) the forces of the division encountered very little resistance and it was perhaps the thick road dust and the unexpectedly warm weather that caused them troubles. By nightfall the spearheads of the 113th were already at the gates of Negotin, outflanking it to the north and south, but the town itself was still firmly in German hands.[104]

101  S. Shtemenko, "The Last Six Months", New York, Doubleday & Company, 1977, pp. 209-211.

102  War diary of 113th Rifle Division. Entry for 28.9.1944. TsAMO, fu. 1312, inv. 1, f. 27, pp. 121-122.

103  The following GHQ units were assigned to the division, thereby turning it into a powerful "shock" group: 35th Guards Mortar Regiment (Katyusha Rocket Launchers), 1202nd Self-Propelled Artillery Regiment (SU-76), 274th Howitzer-Artillery Regiment and one regiment from 3rd Anti-Aircraft Artillery Division.

104  War diary of 113th Rifle Division. Entry for 28.9.1944. TsAMO, fu. 1312, inv. 1, f. 27, pp. 121-122.

Negotin was a hard nut to crack. It was defended by the main body of 1. Mountain Division, known as *Hauptgruppe von Stettner*, totaling ca. 12,000 men, reinforced with elements of the Russian Protective Corps. Nevertheless, the town was taken by the end of 30 September in close cooperation with the Yugoslavian 23rd AVNOJ Division. The actions of Gagen's regular troops and Tito's partisans in that area were further facilitated by the Danube Flotilla, which on 29 September landed a 120-men-strong detachment in Radujevac.

*Marshal Tito and Marshal Tolbukhin, October 1944. (RiP)*

* * *

Contrary to the expectations of the Soviet senior commanders, the initial success of 57th Army in the vicinity of Negotin didn't develop into a breakout and pursuit. The Germans – 1. Mountain Division reinforced with a "Brandenburg" regiment and a battle group of the "Prinz Eugen" Division – put up a spirited resistance and considerably slowed down the offensive of Gagen's 57th Army. The Germans, perhaps, would have been able to inflict even more damage on the attackers, but they gradually began to run out of ammunition.

Tolbukhin was not that much discouraged by the slow progress of Gagen's army, because he knew that the force that would turn the tables was yet to be committed. This was 4th Guards Mechanized Corps, which on 1 October received orders to entrain from Yambol, southeastern Bulgaria, and dispatch for Serbia. While en route to the front, the corps was massively replenished with more the 100 factory-fresh tanks and self-propelled guns.

* * *

During the second week of October 1944 Gagen finally managed to crush the front of Army Detachment "Serbia". Overcoming the stiff German resistance and repelling a number of resolute counterattacks, on 9 October the Soviet and AVNOJ forces captured Klokočevac, Štubik, Rgotina, Zaječar and the vital mining area of Bor. In the vicinity of Žabari the Soviet spearheads reached the valley of the Great Morava River and thus at last broke out of the East Serbian Mountains. With the difficult mountainous terrain already behind them, they were now able to attack Belgrade not only from the northeast, but also from the south.

With the crossing of the East Serbian Mountains, also known as the Serbian Carpathians, ended the first stage of the Belgrade Operation. In the span of 11-12 days, advancing in most difficult conditions, Gagen's troops advanced about 130 km to the northwest. Their opponent, Army Detachment "Serbia", had sustained heavy personnel and materiel losses. The resolute drive of 57th Army also accelerated the operations of its right-hand neighbor, General Rubanyuk's 10th Guards Rifle Corps (46th Army) on the northern bank of the Danube. By 6 October it, in close cooperation with the Yugoslavian partisans, managed to secure a 40-km-long stretch of the riverbank immediately to the northeast of Belgrade. Furthermore, elements of 109th Guards Rifle Division captured a small bridgehead on the southern bank of the Danube in the vicinity of Velko Selo, thereby posing a direct threat on the Yugoslavian Capital from the east.

Upon securing the Klokočevac – Zaječar line 57th Army established tactical cooperation with the divisions of Lieutenant-Colonel Jovanović's 14th Serbian Corps of AVNOJ. They were about to be joined by the main Yugoslavian striking force – 1st Army Group of General Peko Dapčević that would comprise nine divisions. In order to ensure better coordination between the partisans and Gagen's army, a Soviet liaison officer was dispatched to Tito's Supreme HQ in Craiova. Apart from that, Gagen's Chief of Staff, Major-General Verkholovich, regularly visited the command post of Dapčević's 1st Army Group to obtain firsthand information, thereby speeding up the decision-making process.

*A Soviet senior officer and his escort in a German Horch 901 Type 40 staff car have a conversation with some Serbian civilians, October 1944. (RiP)*

\* \* \*

The breakout of the Soviet spearheads into the valley of the Great Morava was definitely an unpleasant surprise for the Germans, on which they were not able to react accordingly. Otherwise, it is difficult to say why they had neglected to reinforce that sector and thus dangerously exposed the southeastern approaches to Belgrade. General Gagen immediately made use of this vulnerability. On 10 October his spearheads forced the river and then continued their drive to the capital.

Marshal Tolbukhin and his aides felt that a fantastic opportunity was unfolding right in front of them. The roadway leading to Belgrade from the south was literally open and undefended. There was no better moment to deliver a coup de main and take the town by direct assault.

Determined to step up the pace of the advance on the Yugoslavian capital, the Marshal ordered the main exploitation force, 4th Guards Mechanized Corps, to be committed to battle on the following morning. Apart from the usual military objectives, a very important political mission was assigned to Gagen and Zhdanov – to "liberate" Belgrade in close cooperation with Tito's partisan formations. By doing this, Stalin definitely intended to show not only the ordinary Serbian people, but also the entire world who is the new ruler of Yugoslavia.

**STRENGTH OF 4TH GUARDS MECHANIZED CORPS (INCLUDING THE TACTICALLY ASSIGNED UNITS AND FORMATIONS), 10 OCTOBER 1944**

- 17,022 men
- 160 T-34 tanks (mostly T-34/85, but also some T-34/76)
- 14 SU-85 self-propelled guns
- 7 ISU-122 self-propelled guns
- 31 BA-64 armored cars
- 34 M3 armored halftracks and Bren carriers
- 145 artillery pieces and AT guns
- 28 howitzers
- 95 AA auto-cannons

- 151 mortars
- 21 BM-13 rocket launchers
- 1,075 motor vehicles and prime-movers
- 49 motorcycles[105]

* * *

The offensive of the joint Soviet-AVNOJ forces seemed unstoppable. On 12 October Zhdanov's tankers, in close cooperation with 1st Proletarian Corps of AVNOJ and the Il-2 Shturmoviks of 17th Air Army, captured Topola. The town, renowned for its beauty, was an important junction situated in the midst of the Šumadija Highland, about 80 km to the south of the Yugoslavian capital. More importantly, its loss meant that the chances of the Gebirgsjäger of 1. Mountain Division to fall back from its present position in orderly fashion, i.e. taking with them all their heavy weapons and equipment, were close to zero, because the main communication line in the area, the Niš – Belgrade highway, was running exactly through Topola. Driven by these considerations, von Weichs urgently deployed in the vicinity of the town the anti-tank battalion of the "Prinz Eugen" Division and a battalion of 117. Jaeger Division, both shipped by rail from Croatia.

Topola was taken from the march already on midday of 12 October by the forward detachment of Zhdanov's corps (36th Guards Tank Brigade reinforced with anti-tank artillery, AA auto-cannons and mortars). Right from the outset it had to deal frequently with German tank-killing groups, usually well concealed and placed in ambush positions. They were made mostly of Flak guns and AFVs accompanied by infantry. During one such engagement, which took place between Topola and Mladenovac, the brigade lost at once five tanks. The leadership of the brigade, however, quickly found a remedy to the situation – the combat teams were instructed to mop up the ambushes with dismounted infantry and concentrated fire of all available weapons. This allowed the detachment to resume its forward movement and secure Mladenovac by the end of the day.

There is little doubt that the tank-killing groups in question were organized around elements of SS-Anti-Tank Battalion 7 of the "Prinz Eugen" Division. This battalion had (as per 30 September 1944) 9 Pak 97/38 7.5 cm anti-tank guns, 12

Flak 2 cm auto-cannons, six 4.7 cm self-propelled anti-tank guns (on Pz I chassis), 2 Semovente da 47/32 self-propelled guns and 9 StuG III assault guns. The latter, actually, were only tactically assigned to the battalion, because were organized as a separate unit designated SS-Panzer-Company 105. It was the ace of that company, the 22-year-old Hauptsturmführer Harry Paletta, who distinguished himself most on that day. He was credited with the destruction of 13 Soviet tanks and later on was awarded the Knight's Cross. (It is difficult to say how many tanks were actually destroyed by Paletta; the records of the brigade show that 15 T-34/85 were lost on 12 and 13 October, ten of which were total write-offs.)[106]

On 13 October the offensive of Zhdanov's corps continued unabated. For the first and only time during the battle of Belgrade the forward detachment was attacked by Luftwaffe. Shortly afterwards it was pounded by artillery, but even this didn't stop the Guardsmen from advancing to the northwest. By midnight the tanks cut off the Smederevo – Belgrade road and by doing so sliced General Müller's group in two. At about 05:00 on 14 October the forward detachment, much to the dismay of the Germans and the locals, broke into the suburbs of the Yugoslavian capital.[107]

Fitzroy Maclean visited the battlefield a couple of days later. He recalls:

It had rained during the night and the lanes were muddy. With the Americans, we had three jeeps between us. Charlie Thayer, Ellery Huntington and an American Sergeant set out in one, Vivian Street and I in another, and Freddie Cole and his two wireless operators in a third. At first we followed country lanes and cart-tracks, between high green hedgerows glistening with raindrops. The fresh, moist landscape, a mixture of greys and browns and greens, had the softness of a watercolor. Entering a village, we found it full of the Red Army. Even in this Slav country the Soviet troops looked strangely outlandish, with their high cheekbones, deeply sunburnt faces and unfamiliar uniforms. But they seemed to be getting on well enough with the local population, laughing and joking with the village boys and girls in a kind of composite Slav language, midway between Serb and Russian. Red flags hung from some of the windows, and at the entrance to the village a triumphal arch of cardboard had been erected in honor of the liberators. Thereafter we came upon Russians at every turn, in large bodies and in small, on foot, on horseback, in carts, trucks, armoured cars and tanks, all moving up

105  TsAMO, fu. 243, inv. 2900, f. 875, p. 131.

106  TsAMO, fu. 3121, inv. 1, f. 25, p. 70.
107  TsAMO, fu. 3121, inv. 1, f. 26, p. 49.

to the front. They were certainly not smart. Their loosely fitting drab-cultured uniforms were torn and stained and bleached by the sun and rain. The clothing of many had been supplemented or replaced by articles of equipment captured from the enemy. Their boots, as often as not, were completely worn out. The individual soldiers were an extraordinary medley of racial types, from the flaxen hair and blue eyes of the Norseman to the high cheekbones, slit eyes and yellow complexion of the Mongol. But they looked as though they meant business. Ragged and unkempt though they might be, their powers of endurance and their physical toughness were self-evident. Their weapons, too, were clean and bright. They gave an indefinable impression of being immensely experienced, self-reliant, seasoned troops, accustomed to being left to fend for themselves and well able to do it.

And all this, no doubt, they were, and more, for they had fought their way here from Stalingrad and the frontiers of Asia, and that fighting, we knew, had been no light matter. Most of them wore two or three campaign medals or decorations, not just ribbons or miniatures, but the full-sized bronze, silver or enameled medals and stars themselves, clinking and jangling on their tunics. Somewhere in my kit I had the large silver and platinum star of the Soviet Order of Kutusov, which had been awarded me some months before, and, seeing that this was an occasion on which decorations were being worn, I dug it out and screwed it on to my battle-dress tunic. This, and the fact that both Charlie and I could talk to them in their own language, had an immediate effect on the Russians, who came crowding round the jeep whenever we stopped, fingering our weapons and equipment admiringly and proudly exhibiting their own.

Scattered over the fields through which we were passing, large numbers of derelict tanks and guns, some blasted by direct hits, others seemingly intact, testified to the violence of the battle which had been raging for the last twenty-four hours and was still in progress. Soviet heavy tanks predominated. In the space of a mile we counted a dozen along the side of the track, their shattered hulks still smoking. Evidently there was still some fight left in the German anti-tank gunners.

Twenty miles or so south of Belgrade we emerged on to the main road and joined a continuous stream of Red Army trucks, tanks and guns flowing northwards into battle. One thing in particular struck us now, as it had struck us from the first, namely, that every Soviet truck we saw contained one of two things: petrol or ammunition. Of rations, blankets, spare boots or clothing there was no trace. The presumption was that such articles, if they were required at all, were provided

at the expense of the enemy or of the local population. Almost every man we saw was a fighting soldier. What they carried with them were materials of war in the narrowest sense. We were witnessing a return to the administrative methods of Attila and Genghis Khan, and the results seemed to deserve careful attention. For there could be no doubt that here lay one reason for the amazing speed of the Red Army's advance across Europe.[108]

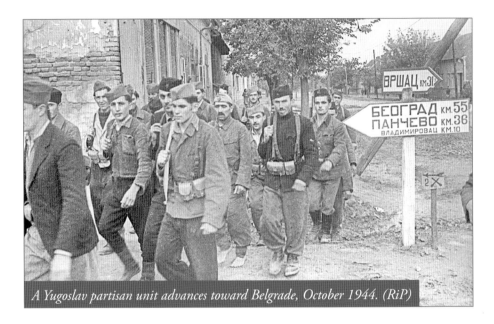

*A Yugoslav partisan unit advances toward Belgrade, October 1944. (RiP)*

## THE DESTRUCTION OF GROUP "STETTNER"

With the road to Belgrade already open, no minute was wasted and the partisans were immediately mounted on the tanks. Facing very little (if any) opposition, the combined detachments of Soviet Guardsmen and AVNOJ troops rushed northwestward and already on 14 October reached the outskirts of Belgrade. There they found themselves in a very puzzling situation. On the one hand, the Yugoslavian capital, the ultimate objective of the entire operation, was now within their grasp.

108  MacLean, op. cit., pp. 504-505.

*Wrecks of vehicles and equipment destroyed during the routing of Group Stettner southeast of Belgrade. 17-20 October 1944. (RiP)*

*Wrecks of vehicles and equipment destroyed during the routing of Group Stettner southeast of Belgrade. 17-20 October 1944. (RiP)*

*Wrecks of vehicles and equipment destroyed during the routing of Group Stettner southeast of Belgrade. 17-20 October 1944. (RiP)*

*Wrecks of vehicles and equipment destroyed during the routing of Group Stettner southeast of Belgrade. 17-20 October 1944. (RiP)*

*Wrecks of vehicles and equipment destroyed during the routing of Group Stettner southeast of Belgrade. 17–20 October 1944. (RiP)*

*Wrecks of vehicles destroyed during the routing of Group Stettner southeast of Belgrade. The StuG III and StuH assault guns displayed in some of the pictures belonged to Assault-Gun Brigade 201. 17-20 October 1944. (RiP)*

*Wrecks of vehicles destroyed during the routing of Group Stettner southeast of Belgrade. The StuG III and StuH assault guns displayed in some of the pictures belonged to Assault-Gun Brigade 201. 17-20 October 1944. (RiP)*

Wrecks of vehicles destroyed during the routing of Group Stettner southeast of Belgrade. The StuG III and StuH assault guns displayed in some of the pictures belonged to Assault-Gun Brigade 201. 17-20 October 1944. (RiP)

On the other hand, there was a wandering German pocket in their immediate rear that was not only threatening their communications, but also was undoubtedly trying to break out and find safety in Belgrade.

To prevent the latter from happening, Marshal Tolbukhin took a decision that was both timely and bold – to break into the city with the main body of 4th Guards Mechanized Corps, and at the same time to turn part of its units to the southeast, thereby completely encircling the "floating" 1. Mountain Division of Generalleutnant Walter Stettner. This move proved to be a complete success. By 17 October a large Axis force, up to 20,000 strong, was trapped in the open field southeast of the city and two days later was completely decimated. Only some of them were lucky to escape death or captivity.

In his memoir, Fitzroy Maclean gives a lively description of what had happened to Stettner's group:

From our new-found friend we learned that in the night a large force of the enemy, which in the confusion of the retreat had become isolated from the main body, had sought to cross the road at about this point in a desperate attempt to fight their way through to join the German garrison in Belgrade before they were finally cut off. The result had been a battle of exceptional ferocity which had raged over this part of the road all night long in the rain and the darkness. Now, the issue was no longer in doubt. Practically the entire enemy force, numbering many thousands had been annihilated. The road was again more or less clear. It only remained to liquidate isolated pockets of resistance. […]

In the knowledge that the road before us was more or less clear, we now continued our journey. Hitherto we had only come upon an occasional dead body, sprawled in the mud beside the wreckage of the tanks and guns. Now corpses littered the sides of the road, piled one on another, some in the field-grey of the Wehrmacht, others stripped of their boots and uniform and left lying half-naked; hundreds and hundreds of them, their pale faces disfigured with mud stains, upon the greenish-grey skin. As we passed, the sickly stench of death struck our nostrils, hanging heavy on the air. The troops who had tried to fight their way out were a composite force, hurriedly thrown together from elements of half a dozen different divisions, and, looking at the dead, we recognized many familiar badges: the Edelweiss of the First Alpine [1. Mountain Division] and the double thunderbolt of the Prinz Eugen. The tables had indeed been turned since we stood opposite these same formations in those early, precarious days in the mountains of Bosnia.

Further along, we passed a great throng of prisoners going in the opposite direction. Many had been left with only their shirts and underpants, and they shivered as they hobbled along in the chilly autumn air, their faces as grey from cold and fear as those of their dead comrades. As we watched, one of the guards appropriated a pair of boots which had somehow passed unnoticed and put them on, leaving their former owner to continue on his way barefoot.

Soon after, Vivian pointed to the side of the road. Looking in the direction in which he was pointing, I saw a hundred or more corpses, lying in rows, one upon the other, like ninepins knocked over by the same ball. They had clearly not died in battle. "A small batch", said Vivian. The smell, sweet and all-pervading, was stronger than ever. [109]

*Yugoslav partisans escort German POWs in Belgrade and its vicinity, October 1944. (RiP)*

---

109 MacLean, op. cit., pp. 507-508.

## LOSSES INFLICTED ON THE ENEMY DURING THE DESTRUCTION OF STETTNER'S FLOATING POCKET, 18-19 OCTOBER 1944 (CLAIMS OF 57TH ARMY)

### Troops, weapons and equipment destroyed
- 5,305 troops
- 30 tanks and self-propelled guns
- 65 artillery pieces
- 49 mortars
- 113 machineguns
- 605 motor vehicles
- 18 prime movers
- 56 motorcycles
- 2,050 horse-drawn carts
- 2,100 horses

### Captured prisoners, weapons and equipment
- 4,887 troops
- 3 tanks
- 180 artillery pieces
- 94 mortars
- 1870 motor vehicles
- 24 prime movers
- 64 motorcycles
- 2,050 horse-drawn carts
- 3,500 horses[110]

\* \* \*

Even though it was partly attributable to tactical circumstances, most of the blame for the destruction of Stettner's group should go to von Weichs. In a directive issued on 14 October the Commander-in-Chief South-East spoke openly about the intention

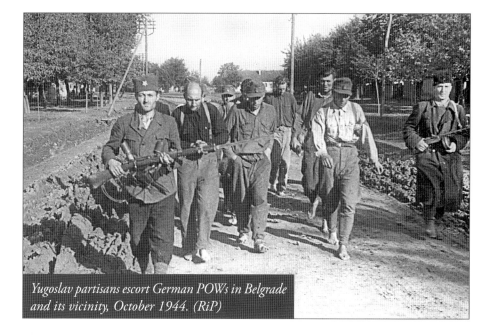

*Yugoslav partisans escort German POWs in Belgrade and its vicinity, October 1944. (RiP)*

of abandoning Belgrade, but at the same time he ordered 1. Mountain Division, which had been cut off and nearly encircled, to join in the battle for the Yugoslavian capital that had started that day, thereby relieving the numerically weak garrison. The possibility of withdrawing the mountain division via Šabac on the Sava, which was located further to the west, was not ruled out, but, according to von Weichs, it depended "on how the operational situation will develop".

The result of this indecisiveness was that in the course of 17 October Group *"Stettner"* (1. Mountain Division — combined with parts of 117. Jaeger Division, Grenadier Brigade 92, a regiment of Brandenburgers and some other units or their parts) made several hopeless and costly attempts to break through the Soviet ring. Stettner didn't issue the order to break out to the west, toward Šabac until the evening, and he himself was mortally wounded in the course of the ensuing fighting. Von Weichs and Felber didn't know the extent of the losses sustained until almost three days later, because the radio transmitter of 1. Mountain Division was not responding. It was only on 21 October, when the vanguards of the largest combat group that had escaped from the pocket (now under the leadership of commander of 117. Jaeger Division *Generalleutnant* August Wittmann) allowed von Weichs to figure out the fatal consequences of his ill-considered directive of 14 October.

110   TsAMO, fu. 413, inv. 10372, f. 400, pp. 29-30.

## ORDER OF BATTLE OF GROUP "STETTNER"
## 17 OCTOBER 1944

- 1. Mountain Division (the main body)
- Grenadier-Brigade (mot.) 92
- 2. Regiment "Brandenburg"
- I. Battalion/4. Regiment "Brandenburg"
- Part of 117. Jaeger-Division (including the division's staff)
- Part of Panzer-Battalion 202

*Obergefreiter* Felhofer of 2. Regiment *"Brandenburg"* was one of those lucky ones who managed to get out of the pocket:

Patrols revealed to us that Belgrade was already occupied by the Russians and that we were encircled. At about 23:00 hours on 17 October 1944 the order came through to destroy as quietly as possible all vehicles and equipment that could not be taken along. Now we realized how far we had to go and began to

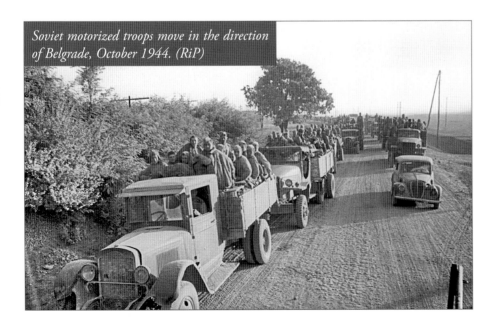

Soviet motorized troops move in the direction of Belgrade, October 1944. (RiP)

suspect what lays ahead of us. Everyone went to work, I smashed up the engine with a pickaxe as best as I could. Then I packed my things and it was difficult to part from my Steyr Kübelwagen with which I had gone through so much. But who had much time for reflection; the Russians had already noticed our work of destruction and sent many salvos in our direction. The ambulances were filled with wounded, lamenting because they knew that there was nothing more our side could do for them. Everyone had to look after himself, all was confusion. Our officers were in action with the companies. There were about 30,000 men in the pocket, but everyone had to find his own way out.

We formed into a group and set out on our own. I had a compass, another a map, behind us a sea of flames, before us uncertainty: how far would we have to go before we reached our main line of resistance, and how we would be able to overcome everything? At best each man was armed with a carbine. Toward town we met up with elements of our company and for us things became easier, because our Hptm. Steidl was there and he had our complete trust. When we reached the main Nish-Belgrade road the Russians were waiting for us. It was still dark and all of a sudden we heard Russian loudspeakers calling for us to surrender. We were told that there were thirty tanks around us and that any attempt to break through would mean certain death. They gave us two hours to think it over.

Many began digging foxholes for protection. They were soldiers from all branches of the Wehrmacht on the run. I crept forward slowly and all went well until I came to a ravine. We must have been noticed, for all of a sudden a real fireworks display began. I got through in one piece again, but every moment someone cried and fell. A few managed to get through this ravine of death, as we called it, and continued in a westerly direction.

At noontime we saw Russians in front of us again. Some tanks roared up and down, and we saw Russian infantry going into position. A Feldwebel from our battalion who spoke perfect Russian had two Panzerfausts, and with these he worked his way up to the Russians. He chased the soldiers from their trenches by calling to them in Russian, and when he was near the tanks he knocked out two. This created confusion among the Russians and we charged, shouting as loud as we could. We had scarcely any ammunition left, but that made us shout all the more. Once again everything worked out, of course many were wounded, bet everyone kept going as best as he could. Our flight continued and we entered a village, where we found something to eat, including some jam. Suddenly we were ordered to fall in. We were ordered to throw away any unnecessary items we still had with us, in order to make it easer to get away. We would have to cover 60 kilometers in the night to come. Then we resumed our flight; rain sprinkled down and it was so dark that it was difficult to see the man in front. Anyone who had on a white shirt tore off a piece and stuck it on the back of the man in front of him so that we did not lose contact. We entered a muddy area; we waded through muck which was knee-deep in places. Many lost their boots but we kept moving irresistibly.[111]

# THE ASSAULT ON BELGRADE

Then came the final act of the Belgrade Operation – the battle for city itself. *Feldmarschall* von Weichs, who providently had moved his HQ to the Croatian town of Vukovar, intended to defend Belgrade at all costs. For that purpose a task force was assembled in a hurry. It comprised elements of several divisions and presumably numbered about 22,000 men, 170 artillery pieces and 40 tanks. Von Weichs hoped that a prolonged battle for the city would tie down considerable enemy forces and by doing so would allow his troops still retreating from the southern part of the Balkans to withdraw undisturbed.

Tolbukhin was aware that Belgrade was well fortified and that's why the attack was planned in a very detailed manner. The battle plan called for a direct assault on the city from the south, on a very narrow sector, towards the riverbank. Then the main forces had to attack in divergent directions, thereby splitting the enemy garrison into fragments and preventing the latter from escaping across the bridges, which had to be taken intact.

*Festung* Belgrade was a hard nut to crack, that's why Tolbukhin had assembled a substantial force along its southern perimeter: 4th Guards Mechanized Corps, three rifle divisions, three artillery brigades, sixteen independent artillery, self-propelled-artillery and mortar regiments, one anti-aircraft artillery division and three independent anti-aircraft artillery regiments. Strong Yugoslavian forces had also been gathered to take part in the liberation of their capital: eight divisions of both 1st Proletarian Corps and 12th Corps.[112]

The offensive also required a close cooperation between the participating Soviet and Yugoslav forces. That's why already on 14 October General Zhdanov (the commanding officer of 4th Guards Mechanized Corps) and the commander of the AVNOJ 1st Army Group met to work out a detailed plan for joint offensive.[113]

**ORDER OF BATTLE OF FORTRESS "BELGRADE" 17 OCTOBER 1944**

- One regiment of 118. Jaeger-Division (less one battalion)
- Assault-Battalion of 2. Panzer-Army
- I. Battalion/1. Regiment "Brandenburg"
- Part of 117. Jaeger-Division
- The bulk of SS-Police-Mountain Regiment 18
- Part of SS-Police Regiment 5
- Part of Alarm-Regiment "Feste Belgrad"
- 1. Battery/Assault-Gun Brigade 191

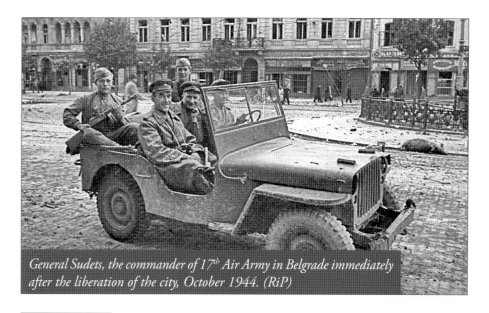

*General Sudets, the commander of 17th Air Army in Belgrade immediately after the liberation of the city, October 1944. (RiP)*

111   H. Spaeter, "The History of the Panzerkorps Grossdeutschland", Vol. 3, Winnipeg: J.J. Fedorowicz Publishing, 2000, p. 98-107.
112   "Istoria na Vtorata Svetovna Voina 1939 - 1945", op. cit., p. 199.
113   Ibid.

*General Sudets, the commander of 17th Air Army in Belgrade immediately after the liberation of the city, October 1944. (RiP)*

\* \* \*

Belgrade was well fortified and prepared for a long-term defense. In several sectors there were anti-tank ditches; concrete bunkers had been built on the main intersections and all main buildings had been turned into strongholds. The defenders possessed considerable firepower (and plenty of light automatic weapons), as well as hand grenades, Panzerfausts and Panzerschrecks. They were also supported by some heavy 8.8 cm Flak guns provided by the Luftwaffe AA units. 114

Special attention was paid to tank-killing. Apart from hand-held anti-tank weapons, the Germans also widely used anti-tank grenades. While fighting against tanks, the defenders always tried to separate them from the accompanying infantry, mainly by firing relentlessly with their machineguns and other weapons. The Germans also tried to trap the T-34s in the narrow streets.

114  TsAMO, fu. 413, inv. 10372, f. 514, pp. 42-42ob.

The Soviets responded to this by forming assault groups heavily supported by guns and mortars. About 70% of the artillery was placed within forward infantry lines and were employed in direct-fire role. Assault engineers were also used in most critical points to storm heavily fortified objects.

The main problem of the garrison was its insufficient manpower strength. Not all endangered sectors could be adequately covered and there were not enough men to escort the AFVs in the street battles.

*Oberfeldwebel* Göller of 3. Company/1. Regiment *"Brandenburg"* describes the fighting in Belgrade in those brutal days:

During the morning of 14 October we received orders to go into position at the east end of the city of Belgrade. The Russians had pulled back from this part of the city at dawn even though they had had no contact with us.

Apparently they were suspicious of the quiet and probably thought it was a trap, even though no one from the German side was there.

At about 14:00 hours we received orders to undertake a counterattack about 800 meters further south, where enemy elements had established themselves at a crossroads.

This area was retaken at nightfall, however we soon discovered that we had been surrounded: elements of 1. and 2. Kp./I./1. Rgt. And I with a few men of the 3. Kp., but with no mortars. The only contact with the battalion command post was by radio. We received orders from the battalion commander, Oblt. Hebler, to make our way to the rail station. The explosions as the rail installations were blown up showed us the way there.

After a terrific night march through houses, backyards, cellars and Russians – our interpreter repeatedly negotiated with them – we finally reached the rail station. There was a brief exchange of fire with the pioneers of the demolition team there who opened fire as soon as our interpreter spoke to them. We soon straightened things out, however, and at daybreak we were warmly welcomed by Oblt. Hebler and a Hauptmann of the commandant's staff. They had already written us off, especially since the Russians were in every part of the city with tanks and strong forces. At about 23:00 hours some of these enemy tanks had made a blind advance out of a single side street. Calling out in German "don't shoot, German tanks!" they then proceeded to shoot up and run over the anti-tank and anti-aircraft guns positioned there. Situated at the intersection had been one 75-mm Pak, 4 anti-aircraft guns, one armored car and ammunition vehicles.

*Destroyed German StuH 42 and M15/42 tanks in Belgrade pictured by a Bulgarian photographer on 5 January 1945. The former probably belonged to 1. Battery/Assault-Gun Brigade 191, the latter – to Panzer-Battalion 202. (Bulgarian Military Photo Archive)*

*A Destroyed German StuH 42 assault howitzer in Belgrade pictured by a Bulgarian photographer on 5 January 1945. The former probably belonged to 1. Battery/Assault-Gun Brigade 191, the latter – to Panzer-Battalion 202. (Bulgarian Military Photo Archive)*

*Destroyed German StuH 42 and M15/42 tanks in Belgrade pictured by a Bulgarian photographer on 5 January 1945. The former probably belonged to 1. Battery/Assault-Gun Brigade 191, the latter – to Panzer-Battalion 202. (Bulgarian Military Photo Archive)*

*A knocked-out Italian-made German M15/42 somewhere in Belgrade, October 1944. (MRNNJ)*

*A knocked-out Italian-made German M15/42 somewhere in Belgrade, October 1944. (MRNNJ)*

*A destroyed German StuG III Ausf. G assault gun (tactical number '131') that presumably belonged to Assault-Gun Brigade 191 on "King Alexander" Boulevard in Belgrade, October 1944. (Author's collection)*

*A destroyed German StuG III Ausf. G assault gun (tactical number '131') that presumably belonged to Assault-Gun Brigade 191 on "King Alexander" Boulevard in Belgrade, October 1944. (Author's collection)*

German troops stand near an Italian-made Autoblinda AB 41 armored car during the opening stages of the battle for Belgrade. 15 October 1944. (Author's collection)

ВРАЧАРСКА

One Russian tank was knocked out by a Panzerfaust. After our resurrection the surviving members of those platoons were incorporated and saw action with us. On 15 October the available part of our battalion (I./1. Rgt.) was formed into assault groups of about twenty men each. These were sent into the heart of this very confused situation (in the southeast area) and assigned to the various sector commanders. The forces there were mainly thrown together alert units made up of sailors, airmen and supply troops, almost all inexperienced in land warfare. My Kampfgruppe and I were assigned as infantry cover to a Leutnant, who was in position at the Belgrade military transmitter with two anti-tank guns. He was in an ideal defensive position behind a small park and from there commanded four intersections. Several enemy tanks had been knocked out from there.

The Leutnant and his crews were very happy to receive us as reinforcements, especially since we knew each other from earlier actions in the Balkans. The park itself was crisscrossed by slit trenches, in which we positioned ourselves. The knocked-out tanks and the feeling of being able to trust one another created a good atmosphere.

Two heavy night attacks against our position were repulsed with the help of anti-tank rifles (they had a terrific effect on the houses!)

The Russians attacked again at dawn and lost two of their tanks to the anti-tank guns. The entire enemy assault was halted, part before the park, part inside. In agreement with the anti-tank guns, we subsequently undertook a counterattack as far as the other end of the park with six men, while the others raked the windows of the houses with submachine-gun and machine-gun fire. We reached the end of the park in one continuous dash. A street separated us from the opposite houses, in which the Russians were sitting. From there, about 40 meters away we could see Russians walking around in an office building with large front windows; it was probably a command post. Two Panzerfaust rounds were fired through the windows; there was a terrible outcry and the Russians came flying out. We were waiting with our machine-guns on the shoulder and four men with submachine-guns. The Russians ran straight into our fire! When the magazine was empty we returned to our start position – with no loss to ourselves. The entire affair had lasted seven minutes at most and had the result that the Russians withdrew from the houses and did not fire another shot in that place all day.

At about 09:00 hours on 16 October Oblt. Hebler came and brought us cigarettes, chocolate and several bottles of champagne from the opened supply dump. Since it was quiet there, we were relieved by about fifty navy and air force soldiers and

after three days and nights were finally able to get some sleep. At about 17:00 hours my group and I were ordered to the high-rise building, as the Russians had already broken through to there with strong forces.

We were able to hold them up though, perhaps because they were surprised to meet resistance; and we were all alone, with no friendly support, no heavy weapons. During the course of the morning of 17 October we withdrew on orders and were received by an alert unit in position at a crossroads further to the rear. Shortly thereafter I was ordered with a squad to the command post , where two heavy mortars were waiting for us. I had to release the squad and search for two mortar crews. By evening I had collected the necessary people, and with plenty of ammunition, radio sets, etc waited for what was to come.

On 18 October we went into position not far from the transmitter, for the park which was so familiar to us had by then changed hands. The alert unit had disintegrated and fled, the brave anti-tank guns had been shot up. The Russians had infiltrated into the trenches in broad daylight and had overrun the entire outfit. The firing position for the two mortars was approximately 80 meters away from the park in a ruin; good field of fire, camouflage and avenue of retreat.

I sited the observation post in the fourth flour of a house, from where there was a good view of the entire park. I took a radio and two runners up with me while one squad from our unit took up position in the lower rooms.

In spite of the close range we soon carried out adjustment fire on the park and were able to fire for effect as if on the practice range. The Russians now put their mortars to use but were unable to root out our firing position; not suspecting us to be so close, they fired too far to the rear.

During the morning the enemy committed strong forces in an attempt to break our resistance, which they failed to do, since each assault into the park collapsed in the fire of our two mortars. Likely encouraged by the mortars, the Kampfgruppen in the neighboring houses also offered spirited resistance.

Inexplicably, at about twelve noon both mortars were put out of action by blockages. Since the crews could not clear the blockages, I decided to go to the firing position myself and repair the damage. I left the runners at the observation post with orders to keep me informed about the enemy and his movements and, if possible, immediately direct fire. On one mortar the striker tip had broken, on the other it was bent. Both were replaced, the barrels quickly cleaned and greased, and firing was resumed immediately using the previous elevation, since the observation post was urgently calling for fire.

Now I wanted to return to my observation post; to do this I had to cross a street which was sometimes in the enemy's view. I aimed for the entrance to the house on the other side, leapt onto the road, and heard the loud bark of a Russian submachine-gun. Hit, I tumbled through the doorway of the house. During the pause in the firing caused by the blockages the enemy had been able to cross the park and get into a house from where he was able to command two further streets. I went to the battalion command post, where my wound was tended to. This was followed by a wild ride across the Save under fire in a motorcycle side-car combination. There I was placed aboard an ambulance train which departed the same evening.

Two days later the city of Belgrade was in Russian hands after a seven-day battle. How many good comrades were killed in that time. My departure from the survivors was difficult, for I sensed that they were facing difficult time.[115]

Soviet infantrymen during the street fighting in Belgrade, October 1944. (RiP)

\* \* \*

The battle for Belgrade was fierce and lasted a full week (from 14 to 20 October). During the first days the Soviets and the Yugoslavs succeeded in driving a deep wedge in the southern perimeter of the fortress. They isolated several pockets of Axis resistance in the southern and eastern limits of the city and subsequently destroyed most of them. But then the joint offensive began to lose momentum, partially because some of the Soviet and AVNOJ troops were redirected to the south to finish off the wandering pocket in their rear (i.e. Stettner's group). The final blow was delivered in the late afternoon of 20 October. Closely cooperating with the friendly air force and the gunboats of the Danube flotilla, the attackers captured the Kalemegdan Fortress, the last German bastion in Belgrade. The remnants of the decimated garrison were evacuated to the northern bank of the Danube.

**LOSSES OF 4TH GUARDS MECHANIZED CORPS DURING THE BELGRADE OPERATION, 12-21 OCTOBER 1944**

- Personnel: 1,491 men (404 KIA, 1,076 WIA and 11 MIA)
- 43 tanks and self-propelled guns
- 6 armored cars
- 8 artillery pieces
- 6 mortars
- 43 motor vehicles[116]

Fitzroy Maclean describes the last hours of the battle for Belgrade:

The Kalemegdan is an ancient fort, built of stone and red brick, from which, in Turkish times, the Ottoman conquerors held sway over Belgrade and the surrounding country. We approached it on foot through what seemed to be some public gardens, having first left the jeeps under the cover of a clump of bushes. As far as we knew, the Kalemegdan itself was in Soviet or Partisan hands, but in the

115 Spaeter, op. cit., pp. 95-98.

116 TsAMO, fu. 243, inv. 2928, f. 67, pp. 42-42ob.

*An Italian-made German M15/42 of Panzer-Battalion 12 abandoned in Niš, mid-October 1944. (Bulgarian Military Photo Archive)*

*An Italian-made German M15/42 of Panzer-Battalion 12 abandoned in Niš, mid-October 1944. (Bulgarian Military Photo Archive)*

An 8.8 cm Flak gun of SS-Flak-Battalion 7 of the "Prinz Eugen" Division captured by the troops of the Bulgarian 2nd Army during the initial phase of its offensive east of Niš, the second week of October 1944. (Bulgarian Military Photo Archive)

An Italian-made German M15/42 of Panzer-Battalion 12 abandoned in Niš, mid-October 1944. (Bulgarian Military Photo Archive)

*Vehicles and equipment of 7. SS-Mountain Division "Prinz Eugen" destroyed during the vigorous attack of the tanks of 1ˢᵗ Bulgarian Armored Brigade at Niš on 14 October 1944. (Bulgarian Military Photo Archive)*

*Guns, vehicles and equipment of 7. SS-Mountain Division "Prinz Eugen" destroyed during the vigorous attack of the tanks of 1st Bulgarian Armored Brigade at Niš on 14 October 1944. (Bulgarian Military Photo Archive)*

*Vehicle of 7. SS-Mountain Division "Prinz Eugen" destroyed during the vigorous attack of the tanks of 1st Bulgarian Armored Brigade at Niš on 14 October 1944. (Bulgarian Military Photo Archive)*

*Vehicle of a Luftwaffe unit destroyed during the vigorous attack of the tanks of 1st Bulgarian Armored Brigade at Niš on 14 October 1944. (Bulgarian Military Photo Archive)*

*Vehicle of 7. SS-Mountain Division "Prinz Eugen" destroyed during the vigorous attack of the tanks of 1ˢᵗ Bulgarian Armored Brigade at Niš on 14 October 1944. (Bulgarian Military Photo Archive)*

*Vehicles and equipment of 7. SS-Mountain Division "Prinz Eugen" destroyed during the vigorous attack of the tanks of 1ˢᵗ Bulgarian Armored Brigade at Niš on 14 October 1944. [The M15/42 tank belonged to Panzer-Battalion 12] (Bulgarian Military Photo Archive)*

*Guns, vehicles and equipment of 7. SS-Mountain Division "Prinz Eugen" destroyed during the vigorous attack of the tanks of 1st Bulgarian Armored Brigade at Niš on 14 October 1944. (Bulgarian Military Photo Archive)*

Vehicle of 7. SS-Mountain Division "Prinz Eugen" destroyed during the vigorous attack of the tanks of 1st Bulgarian Armored Brigade at Niš on 14 October 1944. (Bulgarian Military Photo Archive)

German POWs in Yugoslavia. (Bulgarian Military Photo Archive)

An 8.8 cm Flak gun of SS-Flak-Battalion 7 of the "Prinz Eugen" Division captured by the troops of the Bulgarian 2nd Army during the initial phase of its offensive east of Niš, the second week of October 1944. (Bulgarian Military Photo Archive)

*A knocked-out Pz II Ausf. C light tank of the German 22. Infantry Division found somewhere in Macedonia, October 1944. (Bulgarian Military Photo Archive)*

A knocked-out Pz II Ausf. C light tank of the German 22. Infantry Division found somewhere in Macedonia, October 1944. (Bulgarian Military Photo Archive)

*RSO tractor of the German 11. Luftwaffe-Field Division abandoned in the vicinity of Kumanovo, Macedonia, October/November 1944. (Bulgarian Military Photo Archive)*

immediate neighborhood skirmishing was still in progress and through the trees came the occasional crack of a rifle or a burst of fire from a machine gun. It was not without caution that we wended our way amongst the ornamental flower-beds and clumps of shrubs. 'Keep off the grass', said the notices unavailingly. Suddenly we emerged from the trees on to a kind of terrace and found ourselves looking out over an immense panorama, in which, as in certain medieval paintings, all sorts of things were happening simultaneously. At our feet, a few hundred

*A destroyed Soviet T-34/85 tank of 36th Guards Tank Brigade in front of the Albania Palace in Belgrade, October 1944. (RiP)*

*Yugoslav partisans during the street fighting in Belgrade, October 1944. (RiP)*

120

yards away, flowed the Danube. Here, at the point where it joined the Sava, it was a considerable stream, its rushing waters swollen by the autumn rains. Of the bridges spanning it, only one remained standing, about half a mile from where we stood.

Across this troops were pouring headlong — guns, vehicles, horses and infantry. Looking through our glasses, we saw that they were Germans, retreating in confusion to the suburb of Zemun across the river, where, it seemed, the main body of the enemy was now established and whence their guns were laying

down a barrage to cover the retreat of their rearguard. Suddenly, as we watched, the stream of fugitives was broken, and for a few moments the bridge remained unoccupied. Then more troops came pouring across. As we focused our glasses on them, we saw to our amazement that they were Russians. We could hardly believe our eyes. It seemed incredible that the German sappers should have failed to blow up the bridge as soon as their last troops were across.

And yet there could be no doubt about it. They had. Already the first Russians had reached the other side and were deploying on the flat ground between Zemun and the river. Calmly, methodically, the guns, horse-drawn for the most part, were brought into position and opened up. Little puffs of smoke among the buildings of Zemun showing that they were finding their targets.

Then, as we watched, the Red infantry went into action, wave upon wave, advancing unhurriedly but relentlessly across the shell-scarred fields, firing as they went. Some were armed with tommy-guns or rifles, others dragged behind them heavy machine guns mounted on little wheels. Every now and then one of the

sturdy, buff-clad figures would spin round and fall while the advance swept on past him. On the fringes of Zemun the harassed Germans were standing fast and returning the Russians' fire as they tried frantically to dig themselves in. It was not until later that we heard the story of the bridge. The Germans, it appeared, had duly mined it before they began their withdrawal and a detachment of engineers had been detailed to blow it up as soon as the last troops were over. The rest of the story reads like a fairy tale.[117]

**121**

117  MacLean, op. cit., pp. 510-512.

A destroyed German 8.8 cm Flak 36/37 anti-aircraft gun in Belgrade, October 1944. (RiP)

*A destroyed German 10.5 cm leFH 18/40 howitzer in the outskirts of Belgrade, October 1944. (RiP)*

*A Soviet ZiS-2 57-mm anti-tank gun of 4th Guards Mechanized Corps shells enemy positions in the outskirts of Belgrade. October 1944. (Author's collection)*

*A German Pak 40 7.5 cm anti-tank gun abandoned on Knez Miloš Street, Belgrade, October 1944. Next to it a bunker constructed by the Germans is clearly visible. (Author's collection)*

*captured German Sd.Kfz. 8 prime mover driven by a Soviet soldier in downtown Belgrade, ctober 1944. (Author's collection)*

*A T-34/85 tank of 36th Guards Tank Brigade in Belgrade, October 1944. A BA-64 armored car is in the background. (Author's collection)*

A T-34/85 tank of 36th Guards Tank Brigade in Belgrade, October 1944. A BA-64 armored car is in the background. (Author's collection)

*An Italian-made Autoblinda AB 41 armored car employed by AVNOJ troops, Belgrade, October 1944. (Author's collection)*

*Destroyed T-34/85 tanks of 4th Guards Mechanized Corps on Knez Miloš Street in Belgrade, October 1944. (Author's collection)*

*Soviet T-34/85 tanks of 53rd Independent Motorcycle Regiment replenish with ammunition in the outskirts of Belgrade, October 1944. (Author's collection)*

*Yugoslav partisans stare curiously at a Soviet 45-mm Model 1932 anti-tank gun, Belgrade, October 1944. (Author's collection)*

*A knocked out Italian-manufactured German M15/42 tank in Belgrade, October 1944. Soviet bridge-building equipment in the background. (Author's collection)*

*Opel Blitz trucks of 42nd Anti-Tank Artillery Brigade in Belgrade, October 1944. Both vehicles look brand-new and most probably belong to the "trophies" confiscated from the Bulgarian army. (Author's collection)*

*German troops and Serbian auxiliary forces occupy a defensive position in the vicinity of Belgrade, October 1944. (MRNNJ)*

*The crew of a T-34/85 tank of 36th Guards Tank Brigade (4th Guards Mechanized Corps) is being cheered by local civilians in Belgrade, October 1944. (MRNNJ)*

*A Soviet officer inspects an abandoned German DFS 230 glider in the Belgrade area, October 1944. (Author's collection)*

*Soviet troops inspect a motorcycle. The wreck of a destroyed 2cm Flak 38 auto-cannon is on the foreground. Belgrade, October 1944. (Author's collection)*

*Destroyed T-34/85 tanks of 4th Guards Mechanized Corps on Knez Miloš Street in Belgrade, October 1944. (Rista Marjanović collection)*

# THE BULGARIAN OFFENSIVE

The Bulgarian armed forces joined the Belgrade Operation on 8 October. On their southern flank was positioned 4th Army, which initially was just one-division strong (about 22,000 men with the attached units). Its main opponent was the elite German 22. Infantry Division, which put up a very determined resistance. Therefore, it is not surprising that it took 4th Army nearly a full month to reach the valley of the Varder River in the vicinity of the town of Veles.

Further north operated 1st Army of General Stoichev. Its main assets were two infantry divisions, a parachute battalion and an assault-gun detachment (StuG III). Its task was to block the withdrawal route for Army Group E from Thessaloníki to Skopje.

Stoichev's troops faced the reinforced 11. Luftwaffe Field Division, which had skillfully dug in along the many ridges and valleys in the area. A month of very bloody fighting followed before 1st Army would take Skopje. This took place on 13 November when the divisions marched through the city in triumph.

The strongest of the three armies was 2nd Army of General Stanchev. It was made of five infantry and one cavalry division, plus the armored brigade and an assault-gun detachment. Stanchev's army totaled about 90,000 men, supported by 91 tanks and 760 guns and mortars. Against it von Weichs had deployed the bulk of one of his strongest formations – 7. SS-Mountain Division *Prinz Eugen*.

The offensive of 2nd Army against Niš was in fact a flanking operation that was also aimed at the capture of two other major traffic junctions, Kraljevo, and Priština, which were vital for the withdrawal of the entire Army Group "E".

Stanchev's army encountered very bitter resistance right from the beginning, but, nevertheless, kept pushing forward. The Germans held out till 13 October when 2nd Army finally made some progress. That same day "Prinz Eugen", which was experiencing growing Bulgarian pressure, at last received permission to abandon Niš, with the proviso that the defensive line along the Morava River was to be held for as long as possible. This order was changed shortly afterwards, when *Oberführer* Otto Kumm, the commander of the division, was permitted to withdraw further west, puling one section of his defensive forces at the time. But before long the entire withdrawal turned into a catastrophe.

On the following day (14 October), as a result of delays in constructing a bridge over the Morava, the evacuation of the main body of the 7th SS from Niš became so prolonged that the Bulgarian units pursuing them received the opportunity to achieve a spectacular, albeit unexpected victory. Immediately to the west of the Morava, the armored brigade launched a resolute attack on the flank of the retreating vanguard of the SS division. As result of this swift strike most of the vehicles were destroyed and the survivors were forced to retreat on foot. No precise information on the losses of the division was available at the time. The only thing that Müller and Felber could do was to assume that the losses sustained by the *"Prinz Eugen"* during the withdrawal from the Niš area had exceeded the 5,000 mark.

Lieutenant Radanov, a Pz IV company commander with the Armored Brigade, recalls the lightning action against *"Prinz Eugen"*:

In the morning of 14 October, 2nd Armored Battalion was under strong mortar and assault gunfire. We took position. We started a fire battle with one German 8.8 cm heavy anti-aircraft battery positioned 2km away from us. The battle continued till 2 p.m. At around 2.30 p.m., the commander of the brigade, General Trendafilov, came personally to order the companies and battalion commanders to move towards the road Niš-Prokuplje-Kuršumlja. The aim was to prevent the retreat of the main forces of German *Prinz Eugen* division.

This meant cutting deep into the enemy rear. The task was clear. The idea was understood. At last, we had the opportunity to use the tanks' abilities in the battle. The battalion moved quickly in the direction of Mramor village, aiming for the bridge on the Morava river.

First Armored Battalion was ordered to cover the retreating units deep to the west of Prokuplje.

The vanguard of our battalion was *Poruchik* [Lieutenant] Angelov's armored company, equipped with Škoda light tanks. He became short of fuel about 1km before Mramor village. I replaced him immediately. Reaching 400-500m in front of the village, I saw the following picture: hundreds of motor vehicles mixed with SPA Italian production tanks and anti-aircraft guns moving in the direction of Niš via Mramor towards Prokuplje.

I decided to attack the enemy flank towards the bridge over the Morava River with two platoons and use one platoon frontal on the road. The platoon repositioned in a moving chain. On the left, Poruchik Raychev's 5th Armored Company also repositioned in a chain. At the same time, I informed the Battalion commander *Podpolkovnik* [Lieutenant-Colonel] Bosilkov. He also repositioned the 6th Armored Company of *Poruchik* Cholpanov, which was under his command. I had started the battle while the other companies were still repositioning. To the surprise of

*Serbian peasants stare at the wreck of an Il-2 Shturmovik in the vicinity of Belgrade, October 1944. (Rista Marjanović collection)*

the enemy, I started shooting precisely distributed fire with guns and machine guns. The surprise was effective. Terrified, the enemy started running away. Only two armored fighting vehicles, two 37mm light anti-aircraft guns and two 8.8cm heavy anti-aircraft guns returned fire, but very imprecisely.

Using the fire cover of my company, Raychev's and Cholpanov's tank companies took positions to the left. They fired at the respective targets in front of them, at the same moment the 1st Armored Battalion of *Podpolkovnik* Cenov came from Prokuplje and subsequently the enemy column was surprised at its front as well. The battle was superb. One after another, the vehicles of the enemy were on fire. One after another, guns were silent. Around 4 p.m., any resistance from the enemy was gone. This was the end of the battle on the road Prokuplje-Mramor on 14

October 1944. When night came, the fires of German vehicles lit the battlefield. The use of surprise was an extremely important precondition for the victory at Prokuplje-Mramor.[118]

The offensive of Stanchev's tanks and infantry continued till 30 November, when Kosovo was cleared of Germans and the town of Novi Pazar (in the southeast of Serbia) was taken. By then the withdrawal of von Weichs' forces from Greece, Albania and Serbia had been completed. while Tolbukhin's 3rd Ukrainian Front was approaching Balaton and Budapest.

---

118  Matev, op. cit., p. 234.

*StuG III Ausf. Gs of 2ⁿᵈ Assault-Gun Detachment of the Bulgarian 1ˢᵗ Army in Yugoslavia, October 1944. (Bulgarian Military Photo Archive)*

*A StuG III Ausf. G of 2nd Assault-Gun Detachment of the Bulgarian 1st Army rolls in the direction of the battlefield accompanied by infantrymen, Yugoslavia, October 1944. (Bulgarian Military Photo Archive)*

*A StuG III Ausf. G of 2nd Assault-Gun Detachment of the Bulgarian 1st Army with mounted infantrymen rolls in the direction of the battlefield, Yugoslavia, October 1944. (Bulgarian Military Photo Archive)*

*Loading ammunition in the crew compartment of a StuG III Ausf. G of 2nd Assault-Gun Detachment of the Bulgarian 1st Army, Yugoslavia, October 1944. (Bulgarian Military Photo Archive)*

*A StuG III Ausf. G of 2nd Assault-Gun Detachment and infantrymen of the Bulgarian 1st Army on the streets of Kriva Palanka, Yugoslavia, 10 October 1944. (Bulgarian Military Photo Archive)*

*Refueling of a Bulgarian StuG III Ausf. G.*
*(Bulgarian Military Photo Archive)*

*An RSO tractor of the Bulgarian Armored Brigade loaded with gasoline canisters for the frontline troops, Yugoslavia, the autumn of 1944. (Bulgarian Military Photo Archive)*

*A Maultier half-track truck used by the Bulgarian forces during the operations in Yugoslavia. (Bulgarian Military Photo Archive)*

*An Sd.Kfz. 6 prime mover of the Bulgarian 2nd Army rolls along the Pirot-Bela Palanka road in Yugoslavia, early October 1944. A Renault AHN truck is in the background. (Bulgarian Military Photo Archive)*

*A Pz IV Ausf. H tank of the Bulgarian Armored Brigade moves into position near Poduevo, Yugoslavia, November 1944. (Bulgarian Military Photo Archive)*

*Resting time for the crew of one of the Pz IV Ausf. H tank of the Armored Brigade of the Bulgarian 2nd Army, Yugoslavia, November 1944. (Bulgarian Military Photo Archive)*

*Resting time for the crew of one of the Pz IV Ausf. H tank of the Armored Brigade of the Bulgarian 2nd Army, Yugoslavia, November 1944. (Bulgarian Military Photo Archive)*

*A column of Czechoslovak-made BMM (formerly CKD) LT vz.38 tanks of the Bulgarian Armored Brigade, Sofia, 2 December 1944. (Bulgarian Military Photo Archive)*

*A rear view of Pavesi P4 100 model 30 artillery tractor of Bulgarian 1st Army Artillery Regiment in the mountains of Kumanovo area, Yugoslavia, 6 November 1944. (Bulgarian Military Photo Archive)*

*A Bulgarian 105-mm howitzer towed by an Sd.Kfz 7 prime mover somewhere in the mountains of Yugoslavia, the autumn of 1944. (Bulgarian Military Photo Archive)*

*A Bulgarian VW KDF Typ82 Kübelwagen in Yugoslavia, the autumn of 1944. (Bulgarian Military Photo Archive)*

# SOURCES

**ARCHIVE MATERIAL**
- Bundesarchiv-Militärarchiv, Freiburg: RH 2, RH 10.
- National Archives, Washington D.C.: Microfilmed records series T311, T312, T314, P-035.
- Tsentral'nyi Arkhiv Ministerstva Oborony [Central Archive of the Ministry of Defense of the Russian Federation], Podolsk: various funds.

**PUBLISHED DOCUMENT COLLECTIONS**
- Gryler A. N. et al. (Eds.). Boevoi sostav Sovetskoi Armii. Vol. 3 and 4. Moscow: Voenizdat, 1990.
- Heiber, Helmut and Glantz, David (Eds.). Hitler and His Generals. New York: Enigma Books, 2003.
- Zolotarev V. et al. (Eds.). Velikaia Otechestvennaia Voina. Vol. 16(5-4). Moscow: Terra, 1995 - 2001.

**BOOKS**
- Clark, Alan. Barbarossa. New York: Morrow, 1985.
- Axell, Albert. Stalin's War Through the Eyes of His Commanders. London: Arms and Armour Press, 1997.
- Böttger, Armin. To the Gate of Hell. Barnsley: Frontline Books, 2012.
- Drabkin, Artem. (Ed.) Ya dralsya s Panzerwaffe. Moscow: Yauza-Eksmo, 2007.
- Drabkin, Artem and Sheremet, Oleg. (Eds.) T-34 in Action. Mechanicsburg: Stackpole Books, 2008.
- Duffy, Christopher. Red Storm on the Reich. New York: Da Capo Press, 1993.
- Ganz, A. Harding. Ghost Division. Mechanicsburg: Stackpole Books, 2016.
- Glantz, David M. and House, Jonathan. When Titans Clashed. Lawrence: University Press of Kansas, 1995.
- Grossman, Vasily. A Writer at War. London: The Harvill Press, 2005.
- Guderian, Heinz. Panzer Leader. London: Macdonald Futura Publishers, 1980.
- Hazanov, Dmitriy. Bitva nad Yassami. Avia Master magazine, 4/1999.
- Lipfert, Helmut and Girbig, Werner. The War Diary of Hauptmann Helmut Lipfert. Atglen: Schiffer Publishing, 1993.
- Loza, Dmitriy. Commanding the Red Army's Sherman Tanks. Lincoln: The University of Nebraska Press, 1996.
- MacLean, Fitzroy. Eastern Approaches. London: Jonathan Cape, 1949.
- Mariinskiy, Evgeniy. Red Star Airacobra. Solihull: Helion & Company, 2006.
- Matev, Kaloyan. The Armoured Forces of the Bulgarian Army 1936-45. Solihull: Helion & Company, 2015.
- Miller, Marshall Lee. Bulgaria During the Second World War. Stanford: Stanford University Press, 1975.
- Mladenov, Alexander; Andonov, Evgeni and Grozev, Krassimir. The Bulgarian Air Force in the Second World War. Solihull: Helion & Company, 2018.
- Rudel, Hans-Ulrich. Stuka Pilot. New York: Bantam Books, 1984.
- Shtemenko, Sergei. The Last Six Months. New York: Doubleday & Company, 1977.
- Spaeter, Helmuth. The History of the Panzerkorps Grossdeutschland. Vol. 3. Winnipeg: J.J. Fedorowicz Publishing, 2000.
- Trevor-Roper, Hugh. Hitler's Table Talk, 1941-1944. New York: Enigma Books, 2000.
- Wacker, Albrecht. Sniper on the Eastern Front. Barnsley: Pen & Sword, 2005.
- Werth, Alexander. Russia at War 1941-1945. New York: E. P. Dutton & Co, 1964.
- Wood, Ian Michael. Tigers of the Death's Head. Mechanicsburg: Stackpole Books, 2013.
- Ziemke, Earl F. Stalingrad to Berlin: The German Defeat in the East. Washington D.C.: Office of the Chief of Military History, United States Army, 1968.
- - . Istoria na Vtorata Svetovna Voina 1939 - 1945. Vol. 8 and 9. Sofia: Voenno izdatelstvo, 1980.
- - . Sovetskie Voenno-vozdusnye sily v Velikoi Otechestvennoi voine 1941 - 1945. Moscow: Voenizdat, 1968.
- - . Velikaya Otechestvennaya Voina 1941 - 1945. Vol. 3. Moscow: Nauka, 1999.